Trusting God In Trouble Times

Unless otherwise noted, all scriptural citations are taken from the Authorized (King James, Message and Amplified) Version of the Bible.

ISBN: 978-0-9963430-5-3

I0169596

Kesza
PUBLISHING, LLC

KESZA Publishing LLC
P.O. Box 1295
Marrero, LA 70073

If this book has been a blessing to you, please send

us your testimony to kwa@kwa.life

ACKNOWLEDGEMENTS

I give honor and thanks to God for His Holy Spirit who is within me, teaching me, and guiding me through awesome projects like this and others. He is my source of inspiration.

Thanks to my lovely wife, Ethel C. Antoine, for your continued support and dedication throughout the years. We have been life mates and partners for over twenty years now. I look forward to the next twenty years.

Thanks to my children, Seth and the late Zachary. You have been the joy of my life, and teaching you, and watching you grow have been exciting. God has wonderful love for you and plans for you.

Much love to my wonderful and faithful congregation of Royal Palace Ministries and the partners of KWA International. We have been

through much together and conquered all. I love

you all, and you are by far the best group of people

in this world!

Trusting God In Trouble Times

Twelve Tangible Ways

To Trust God

Trusting God In Trouble Times

Introduction

There are times in our lives when things just don't seem right. We find ourselves faced with all sorts of obstacles. There are things that happen in our lives that are out of our control. What do you do when things go wrong? What do you do when you're faced with obstacles that you did not cause? How do you handle problems that arise? Where do you go when you don't know what to do? It is my prayer that this book will be a source of information that can help you navigate through life's ups and downs. It is the purpose of this book to provide you with information that can help you to trust God in trouble times. As you read from chapter to chapter, I will provide you with information that can help you navigate issues that arise in your life that seem out of your control. I believe that no matter what life throws at us, there is a way that we can trust God as we figure out how to handle it. Let's take a journey through the pages of this book and discover that just because we may be surprised by life, we don't have to be in a panic or filled with anxiety and worry. We can face life's issues good and bad and at the same time, trust God. Let me give you twelve tangible ways you can learn how to trust God in trouble times.

Chapter One

Truth Matters

Trusting God In Trouble Times

The word truth means unconcealed, manifest, and to be genuine. It is this truth that we must come to know personally. It is only when we embrace this truth that life will take on a whole new meaning and direction. I'm talking about Jesus Christ. The Bible says in the book of John 1:17, "For the law was given by Moses, *but* grace and truth came by Jesus Christ." It says that truth came by Jesus. That means that truth is not a thing but a person, and that person is Jesus Christ.

I'm telling you this because we live in a world where truth doesn't really matter anymore. You're told to lie and steal just to get ahead, and it really doesn't matter who you destroy on the way up as long as you're satisfied. Always remember this -

truth matters.

If you are going to trust God in trouble times, you

are going to have to know the truth. The truth is

something you can stand on, something that comes

with the full force of God backing it. Decide today

that no matter where life finds you, and no matter

what you are dealing with, that you're going to

embrace this truth that God speaks in His word.

Listen to what Jesus says in the book of

John 8:31-32.

Then said Jesus to those Jews which believed on
him, If ye continue in my word, *then* are ye my
disciples indeed; And ye shall know the truth, and
the truth shall make you free.

John 8:31-32 (King James Bible)

Notice in John 8:31, Jesus says that if you continue in His word, you are His disciple; and, by being his disciple, you shall know the truth and the truth shall make you free. This is important because Jesus is the truth, and to become a learner of Him and a disciple of His, there can only be the truth, for Jesus cannot lie and will never lie. So, when you partner with Him, you are undergirded with truth.

Having said that, it is also important to know that you can trust the truth that comes from Jesus. When I say trust, I'm talking about confidence or faith in a person or thing; to believe; to expect; to entrust; to depend on. And this trust is as equally as important as the truth because the truth is, you can trust Him. There is something else that I need to mention here, and that is confidence.

Confidence is a feeling of self-assurance; a feeling of trust in a person; reliance and good faith. This is important because you are not only being asked to be His disciple, but to trust Him for the truth and to have confidence in Him that what He says is reliable.

There are some benefits that come with trusting Jesus and trusting His word. Let me give you a few of these benefits that you can rely on when you come to a place of trusting Jesus and believe that truth matters:

THE BENEFITS OF TRUSTING

➢ **Direction- ISA. 30:21, 42:16**

- ➢ **A Full Storage- PS. 31:19**

- ➢ **Unfailing Love- PS. 32:10**

- ➢ **Redemption- PS. 34:22, ISA. 12:2**

- ➢ **Unmovable- PS. 125:1**

- ➢ **Safety- Pr. 29:25, ISA. 50:10**

- ➢ **Peace- ISA. 26:3,4**

- ➢ **Blessed- JER. 17:7,8, PS. 115:9-15**

It is important to decide today that truth matters, and to be a truth seeker. You're going to govern your life by truth. This is important because if you are truly going to trust God, you are going to have to learn that His word is true, and that it is His word that will be the foundation of your life no matter what this world says and no matter what is going on around you. You are determined to trust God and His word as truth.

This is what Jesus says in the book of John 17:17, "Sanctify them through thy truth: thy word is truth."

Jesus is saying that it is His desire that God would sanctify His disciples and you through His truth, and then He says His word is truth. Jesus and His word, which is true, are synonymous; you cannot have one without the other because He is the word, and the word is Him. He is truth, and truth is Him. Again, listen to what Jesus says in John 14:6, "Jesus saith unto him, I am the way, the truth, and the life: no man cometh unto the Father, but by me."

Trusting God In Trouble Times

Now that we have established that truth matters and that truth can only be found in the word of God, you are now ready to truly trust God in trouble times.

Now let's get deeper into His word so that you can see and discover what it says about trusting God in trouble times.

Chapter Two

Tangent Moment

Trusting God In Trouble Times

I love what the Bible says in the book of Proverbs 3:5-8. It says trust God from the bottom of your heart; don't try to figure out everything on your own, and listen for God's voice in everything you do. Everywhere you go, He is the one who will keep you on track. Don't assume that you know it all. Run to God! Run from evil! Your body will glow with health, and your very bones will vibrate with life.

Wow, what a promise! God is not only saying that truth matters, but He is also suggesting to us that we need to truly trust Him; and to do that properly, we must have what I call a tangent moment. That is a sudden change from one course to another. You may have trusted in finances, jobs, and people, but you need to decide today that you're

going to change from trusting in things and people

to trusting in God.

It is then that you will have what I call a tangent

moment. Listen to what the Bible says in the book

of Psalms 41: 1-3.

To the Chief Musician, A Psalm of David.
Blessed *is* he that considereth the poor: the LORD
will deliver him in time of trouble. The LORD will
preserve him, and keep him alive; *and* he shall be
blessed upon the earth: and thou wilt not deliver
him unto the will of his enemies. The LORD will
strengthen him upon the bed of languishing: thou
wilt make all his bed in his sickness.

Psalm 41:1-3 (King James Bible)

Psalms 41 says that when you consider the weak

and the poor, the Lord will deliver you in times of

evil and trouble. It says that the Lord will protect

you and keep you alive. He shall call you blessed, and you will not be delivered to your enemies. The Lord will substantially refresh and strengthen you on your bed of affliction.

It also says that the Lord will turn, change, and transform you from being sick or in trouble to being blessed. You can call this a tangent moment - a moment when you go from one condition to another. You see, this is what God provides for His people.

It also says in Psalm 138: 7-8, "Though I walk in the midst of trouble, You will revive me; You will stretch out Your hand against the wrath of my enemies, and Your right hand will save me."

Trusting God In Trouble Times

The Lord will perfect that which concerns me; Your mercy and loving-kindness, O Lord, endure forever- forsake not the works of Your own hands.

God is so good that there are tangent moments in your life provided by Him, and those are moments that He brings you from one bad situation to a better situation. I'm telling you that if you are going to trust God in trouble times, you must decide in your mind that you are going to move from trusting in other things and people to trusting in God. God is the One Who sustains you, protects you, and provides for you, even in the midst of calamities and crisis. He is the One Who you can depend on no matter what.

Trusting God In Trouble Times

Let's look at II Corinthians 1:3 and see another

promise of comfort and care that God promises to

you.

Blessed *be* God, even the Father of our Lord Jesus
Christ, the Father of mercies, and the God of all
comfort; Who comforteth us in all our tribulation,
that we may be able to comfort them which are in
any trouble, by the comfort wherewith we
ourselves are comforted of God. For as the
sufferings of Christ abound in us, so our
consolation also aboundeth by Christ. And whether
we be afflicted, *it is* for your consolation and
salvation, which is effectual in the enduring of the
same sufferings which we also suffer: or whether
we be comforted, *it is* for your consolation and
salvation. And our hope of you *is* stedfast,
knowing, that as ye are partakers of the sufferings,
so *shall ye be* also of the consolation. For we
would not, brethren, have you ignorant of our
trouble which came to us in Asia, that we were
pressed out of measure, above strength, insomuch
that we despaired even of life: But we had the
sentence of death in ourselves, that we should not
trust in ourselves, but in God which raiseth the
dead: Who delivered us from so great a death, and
doth deliver: in whom we trust that he will yet
deliver *us;* Ye also helping together by prayer for

us, that for the gift *bestowed* upon us by the means of many persons thanks may be given by many on our behalf.

II Corinthians 1:3-11 (King James Bible)

I want you to see in the Scriptures that no matter what you go through in life, there is a promise from God that He would never leave you, nor will He forsake you.

As you can see, Paul the writer of this book, is explaining to the Corinthian church that no matter what situation he found himself in, because he was a disciple of Jesus Christ and he trusted in Jesus, that he was suffering because of the gospel. He tells them that in the midst of his suffering, God comforts, consoles, and encourages him as well as them in every trouble and calamity or affliction.

Paul is telling them this so they would be able to understand that even though they find themselves in trouble, they can be assured that they will also be able to comfort, console, and encourage others who may come after them. And, they can experience similar troubles or distress with the comfort that they themselves have been comforted. You see, I know it may seem hard to fathom this thought, but consider this, never waste trouble and always look for the lesson that can be extracted from every calamity, trouble, or affliction that you experience.

This is why Paul goes on in his letter to the Corinthian church to tell them about Christ's own sufferings. He says Christ's comfort, consolation, and encouragement are also shared abundantly by them. He says today if they are troubled, afflicted, and distressed, it is for their comfort, consolation, and encouragement. He is telling them that if they trust God in the midst of what they're going through, they can learn a lesson and then turn around and use that lesson to help somebody else because ultimately, trusting God in trouble times can be useful. You just have to have a tangent moment when you change the way you see trouble, and you move from being troubled by trouble and allow the trouble to teach you lessons that you can turn around and help somebody else.

It sounds far-fetched and almost ludicrous to tell you that you can find lessons in these trouble times when all you want to do is to scream. I get it.

Trouble happens to all of us. But, what I'm trying

to convince you of is, by trusting God in trouble

times and trusting that His word is true, and when

you no longer handle trouble the same, you've had

a tangent moment.

Instead of panicking, living in fear, and being

filled with anxiety, you have a new mindset; and,

that mindset is that you now trust God no matter

what it looks like or feels like. You believe in your

heart that God is with you and for you, and no

matter what comes up against you, you can now

say, "I got this."

Chapter Three

Tower Move

What is a tower move? What am I saying when I ask you to make a tower move?

If you are going to trust God in trouble times, you must move your trust from every high place that you have placed it and move it back to God. This tower move is putting your trust permanently in God.

Salvation Move

If you have never been born again, or you have never accepted Jesus Christ as your Lord and Savior, then the first move that you need to make is to trust His finished work on the cross and to believe in your heart and to confess with your mouth that Jesus came and lived a sinless life and died upon the cross for your sins. By accepting His finished work on the cross, you are receiving Him as your Lord and Savior.

If you have done that already, but for some reason you walked away from Him and no longer trust that He can provide for and protect you, and the fellowship has been broken, then you simply have to move back to Him.

This is what I'm saying - to make a tower move is to place your life in the hands of a higher power, and that source is the Savior Jesus Christ Himself. There is none higher than Him.

Taking Refuge In Him

I want you to look at the word refuge as an acronym (R.E.F.U.G.E); what I want you to remember is this: Receiving Everything From

Under God Every day.

Every time you see the word refuge, I want you to

say that acronym and put yourself in the mindset

that you are receiving everything from under God

every day. By doing this, you are literally making

Him your refuge and your high tower - a place of

safety.

Let us look at Psalm 91 and see what the Bible

says concerning God being our refuge.

HE WHO dwells in the secret place of the Most
High shall remain stable and fixed under the
shadow of the Almighty [*Whose power no foe can
withstand*]. I will say of the Lord, He is my Refuge
and my Fortress, my God; on Him I lean and rely,
and in Him I [*confidently*] trust! For [*then*] He will
deliver you from the snare of the fowler and from
the deadly pestilence. [*Then*] He will cover you
with His pinions, and under His wings shall you
trust and find refuge; His truth and His faithfulness

are a shield and a buckler. You shall not be afraid
of the terror of the night, nor of the arrow (the evil
plots and slanders of the wicked) that flies by day,
Nor of the pestilence that stalks in darkness, nor of
the destruction and sudden death that surprise and
lay waste at noonday. A thousand may fall at your
side, and ten thousand at your right hand, but it
shall not come near you. Only a spectator shall you
be [*yourself inaccessible in the secret place of the
Most High*] as you witness the reward of the
wicked. Because you have made the Lord your
refuge, and the Most High your dwelling place,
There shall no evil befall you, nor any plague or
calamity come near your tent. For He will give His
angels [*especial*] charge over you to accompany
and defend and preserve you in all your ways [*of
obedience and service*]. They shall bear you up on
their hands, lest you dash your foot against a stone.
You shall tread upon the lion and adder; the young
lion and the serpent shall you trample underfoot.
Because he has set his love upon Me, therefore
will I deliver him; I will set him on high, because
he knows and understands My name [*has a
personal knowledge of My mercy, love, and
kindness--trusts and relies on Me, knowing I will
never forsake him, no, never*]. He shall call upon
Me, and I will answer him; I will be with him in
trouble, I will deliver him and honor him. With
long life will I satisfy him and show him My
salvation

Trusting God In Trouble Times

Psalm 91:1-16 (Amplified Bible)

I want you to notice what the Bible says in Psalm 91:1. It says, "He Who dwells in the secret place of the Most High shall remain stable and fixed under the shadow of the Almighty, Whose Power no foe can withstand." The key word in this Verse is dwells. This word literally means to sit down. Yes, that's right - to sit down. That is a picture of rest when you decide to trust God by making Him your hiding place, your high place, and your healthy place;

You must determine in your mind to sit down. It is in this position of rest that mentally your body can recuperate and release the toxicity that has built up because of fear, anxiety, and worry.

It also means to sit in quiet. That is a peaceful state, and whenever we allow our minds to rest in such a way, it calms our surroundings and welcomes peace to come in.

I would encourage you right now to take a deep breath, to sit down, and to keep quiet for a moment. Just take it all in and just enjoy being in the presence of the Lord. Allow His grace to fall over you like a waterfall rinsing away all of the dirt and filth of this world. Allow His grace to minister to you as you sit in a quiet place trusting that no matter what you're facing right now, God has you.

Trusting God In Trouble Times

I want you to remember this, whenever you are at work; God is resting, and whenever you are resting, God is at work.

Let me tell you the story about a woman named Ruth, who was married to Naomi's son. One day Ruth husband died, and she decided that she would continue to live with Naomi. Wherever Naomi went, Ruth decided to go.

You can find the story in the book of Ruth 3:18. Naomi instructed Ruth to sit and rest until the matter was fixed..

Ruth was always going in the field to work so she could bring home food. It says in that verse, "Wait my daughter, until you find out what happens. For the man will not rest until the matter is settled today." Naomi is telling Ruth, sit and rest. You've done everything you can do naturally, now sit and rest. In this story, Naomi is a type of Holy Spirit, Ruth represents you, and Boaz represents Jesus. So in essence, Naomi, which is the Holy Spirit, is telling you to rest, sit, and be at peace until Christ works out the problem.

This is exactly what God is telling you right now. He is telling you to sit and listen . I understand what you're going through. I know where you are, I know what you are facing, and I am well acquainted with your situation; but, what I want you to do is to sit and be at rest while I work things out.

I also want you to notice that it says in Psalm 91: 2 that the Lord is your refuge. Remember, I told you in previous chapters that God is our refuge. I want to give you an acronym for the word refuge again. Whenever you look at the word refuge, I want you to say this: receiving everything from under God every day. Every time you see the word refuge, I want you to be reminded that you receive everything from under God every day.

In verse 3 He says He will deliver you from the snare of the fowler and from the deadly pestilence. This is a promise from God that it is His desire that you be healed in this healthy place. The Bible tells us in several places that by Jesus's stripes we are healed. It tells us in Isaiah 53:5 that by His stripes we are healed. It also tells us in I Peter 2:24 but by His stripes you were healed. You see, when you trust the finished work of Jesus Christ on the cross and you come to a place not of toiling, not of panic, but a peaceful place where you can simply sit down and rest, it is a place where you can receive from God instead of worrying about what to give God.

Now, this may sound far-fetched, but listen. We serve a God who wants to give unto us, not just receive from us. Remember, God promises that we should not be afraid of the terror by night, nor of the arrows by day, nor of the pestilence that stalks in darkest. It says that 1,000 may fall at your side and 10,000 at your right hand, but the key here is that it says it shall not come near you because you are in a high place. You are in a hidden place; and, yes, you are in a healthy place. Can I get you to shout hallelujah to the Most High God for the things that He has done?

Finally; listen to what Psalm 91:10 says. There shall no evil befall you, nor any plague or calamity come near your tent. That is a promise that when you are in this high place in Christ, the enemy cannot find you, and when you are in this hidden place in Christ, the enemy cannot find you, and when you are in this healthy place, no plague and no calamity shall come near you. These are the promises of your Father given unto you; and, what I want you to do now is to continually read Psalm

91, and all of the other scriptures that are in this book, and saturate your mind with His promises concerning your protection and your healing, and not just your protection, but the protection of your whole family.

I want you to read these decrees and declarations out loud and let them saturate your heart and mind:

Psalm 91 Decree & Declarations

- **I DECREE AND DECLARE THAT I WILL DWELL IN THE SHELTER OF THE MOST HIGH GOD!**
- **I DECREE AND DECLARE THAT I WILL FIND REST IN THE SHADOW OF THE ALMIGHTY!**
- **I DECREE AND DECLARE THAT GOD IS MY REFUGE AND MY FORTRESS!**
- **I DECREE AND DECLARE THAT YOU ARE MY GOD, IN WHOM I TRUST AND WITH GREAT CONFIDENCE IN WHOM I WILL RELY!**

- **I DECREE AND DECLARE THAT GOD WILL RESCUE ME FROM EVERY TRAP AND PROTECT ME FROM EVERY DISEASE!**

- **I DECREE AND DECLARE THAT I AM COVERED AND PROTECTED BY HIS OUTSTRETCHED ARMS!**

- **I DECREE AND DECLARE THAT GOD'S FAITHFUL PROMISES ARE MY ARMOR AND PROTECTION!**

- **I DECREE AND DECLARE THAT I WILL NOT BE AFRAID OF THE TERRORS OF THE NIGHT, NOR OF THE ARROWS THAT FLY IN THE DAY!**

- **I DECREE AND DECLARE THAT I WILL NOT DREAD ANY DISEASE THAT STALK IN THE DARKNESS, NOR ANY DISEASE THAT STRIKES AT MIDDAY!**

- **I DECREE AND DECLARE THAT BECAUSE GOD IS MY REFUGE AND THE ALMIGHTY GOD OF MY HOME, NO EVIL CAN BEFALL ME, AND NO PLAGUE CAN COME NEAR MY DWELLING!**

- **I DECREE AND DECLARE THAT GOD HAS ORDERED HIS ANGELS TO**

GUARD, DEFEND, AND PROTECT ME AND MY HOUSE!

- **I DECREE AND DECLARE THAT GOD'S ARMIES OF HEAVEN WILL KEEP ME FROM FALLING; I WILL WALK UNHARMED AND KICK ANYTHING THAT IS EVIL FROM MY PATH!**

- **I DECREE AND DECLARE THAT BECAUSE OF GOD'S LOVE FOR ME, I WILL CALL UPON HIM, HE WILL SET ME ABOVE ALL MY TROUBLES, HE WILL DELIVER ME FROM ALL OF MY FEARS, AND HE WILL HONOR ME WITH HIS PRESENCE AND POWER!**

- **I DECREE AND DECLARE THAT HE WILL REWARD ME WITH LONG LIFE; I SHALL LIVE AND NOT DIE, AND HE WILL SHOW ME HIS SALVATION!**

I want you to read this to yourself on a daily basis and to comfort your heart and your mind with the promises God made to you in Psalms 91.

Trusting God In Trouble Times

The Bible also says in the book of Psalm 9:9-10 that the Lord also will be a refuge and a high tower for the oppressed, a refuge and a stronghold in times of trouble, high cost, destitution, and desperation; and, they who know Your name, who have experience and acquaintance with Your mercy, will lean on and confidently put their trust in You, for you Lord, has not forsaken those who seek, inquire of, and for You on the authority of God's Word and the right of their necessity.

Notice that it said that the Lord is not only a refuge. Remember, we said when you see the word refuge to use it as an acronym and say I am receiving everything from under God every day, and remember that He is also a high tower.

The word for refuge in this amplified translation means a cliff or an inaccessible place.

I want you to begin to trust God. He says you can run to Him, and He will protect you. I want you to trust His word as the truth and to have a tangent moment where you turn to Him.

Chapter Four

Tailor & Train Mentality

I want you to pay close attention to this quote by Carl Jung. "Until you make the unconscious conscious, it will direct your life, and you will call it fate."

This is the point where not only must you trust God's word as being true, and not only must you have a tangent moment where you change from one thing to another, and not only must you have a tower move, but this is the most important process of them all, because it is now that you consider tailoring and training your mind.

Now I do not want you to look at all of the things that I am giving you to trust God in trouble times as a to do list that causes your life to spin out of control with rules and regulations, bringing your spirit to a place of toiling. Instead, I need you to relax and to take a deep breath and to receive these tangible and practical principles with the spirit of receiving through grace.

Remember, grace is the unearned, unmerited, and undeserved favor from God; and, although we have a part to play in the process, it is not a part that causes us to panic, to live in fear, or to live a life full of anxiety. Rather, trust that what His word promises us is already ours to enjoy. All we have to do is believe it and receive it, and so it is necessary in this chapter as I begin to show you how to tailor and train your mentality that you prepare yourself to change the way you think. Remember the quote, "until you make the unconscious conscious, it will direct your life, and you will call it fate."

Let me give you the definition for the word fate. It means something that is unavoidable befalls a person; fortune; lot, the universal principle or ultimate agency by which the order of things is presumably prescribed; the decreed cause of events; time that which is inevitably predetermined; destiny; a prophetic declaration of what must be: death, destruction, or ruin.

So as you can see, the word fate means that things will happen out of your control that you are not responsible for - life has already determined what will happen to you. This could not be further from the truth. I need you to really listen to what I am

about to say. It will literally change your life. Life
is not lived by the determination of an outside
source, or mother nature, or some predestined
thing that happens without your participation. I do
believe in the purpose and will of God for our lives
but not without our participation. You see, God has
given all of us something called a free will, and it
is this will that serves as a gatekeeper to our minds
and thoughts.

Let's first look at Romans 12 beginning with verse
1, and see what the Bible says as it relates to our
life.

I beseech you therefore, brethren, by the mercies
of God, that ye present your bodies a living
sacrifice, holy, acceptable unto God, *which is* your
reasonable service. And be not conformed to this
world: but be ye transformed by the renewing of
your mind, that ye may prove what *is* that good,

and acceptable, and perfect, will of God.

Romans 12:1-3 (King James Bible)

Romans 12:1 shows us that God is, in a sense, asking us to present our bodies as a sacrifice and to be pleasing to Him. He says do not be conformed to this world, but be transformed by the entire renewing of your mind.

Now I like the amplified version of this Scripture which says, "I appeal to you therefore, brethren, and beg of you in view of all the mercies of God to make a decisive dedication of your bodies presenting all your members as a living sacrifice holy devoted, consecrated and well pleasing to God, which is your reasonable, rational, intelligent service and spiritual worship."

It goes on to say in verse 2, (which is extremely important), "Do not be conformed to this world, this age, fashioned after and adapted to its external, superficial customs, but be transformed, changed by the entire renewal of your mind, by its new ideals and its new attitude, so that you may prove for yourselves what is the good and acceptable and perfect will of God, even the thing which is good and acceptable and perfect in His sight for you." The key here is that if you are going to live a life according to His word - a purposeful life, a life filled with joy and peace - you will have to change your mind. You will have to tailor and train your mentality.

The Belief System- What Is It?

What is your belief system and what does it mean to say belief system? Belief system is a set of ideas, thoughts, and opinions and ways that you have.

Where did they come from? The time you were born and you learned to walk, you learned to talk, and you learned various things of life. Your belief system was being shaped. The way that you see life. It is the way that you navigate through life, and it is how you make decisions. It is how you perceive things to be. A belief system is extremely important.

Let me show you a story in the Bible to help

explain how important your belief system is in the

book of Mark 9 starting with verse 18.

There was a man who had a son, and his son was

filled with an evil spirit. The evil spirit often threw

the young man in the fire. It threw him down to the

ground, causing him to convulse. The man brought

his son to Jesus's disciples in order for them to

heal him, but Jesus's disciples. were unable to cast

the demons out of the young man. The father then

decided to bring his son to Jesus.

Jesus's reply is shown in verse 19, and He

answered them, "O unbelieving generation without

any faith! How long shall I have to do with you?

How long am I to bear with you? Bring him to

me." Look at Jesus's response to the father's son in verse 20. It says they brought the boy to Him and when the spirit saw Him, at once it completely convulsed the boy; and he fell to the ground and kept rolling about foaming at the mouth. And Jesus said to his father, "How long has he had this?" He answered, from the time he was a little boy. And it has often thrown him both into fire and into water, intending to kill him.

He asked Jesus if He could do anything have pity on us and help us?

I want you to pay close attention to what Jesus's response was. Listen to what Jesus says in verse 23. Jesus said, "you say to Me, If You can do anything? Why all things can be possible to him who believes." At once the father of the boy gave

an eager piercing cry and with tears and he said,

"Lord, I believe! constantly help my weakness of

faith."

In another translation it says to help my unbelief.

To believe or to have belief simply means to be

confident, to have faith, or trust in the possibilities.

It is to simply believe that Jesus has the power to

do what you're asking Him to do. So when I say

the belief system and ask what is it again, it is all

of the information that you have accumulated

down through the years that have shaped the way

you think and the way you believe. This is so

crucial because whenever you are about to make a

decision and whenever you are about to decide one

way or the other, it is your belief system that determines how you see it, what do you think about it, and how did you handled it in the past. Since we realize that our belief system sets the way that we react to crises, emergencies, and situations, it is imperative that we make some changes to our belief system. For example, maybe the way that you handle a crisis is to become paranoid.

What is paranoid and what does it mean to be paranoid? Paranoid is a mental insanity marked by systematic delusion.

Your belief system in your subconscious mind tells your conscious mind to panic and to handle the situation in a state of frenzy, so it is important that we reset the belief system and to move from a paranoid state so you would be able to trust God in trouble times.

This can be accomplished by our second point and that is the biology of belief. Understanding how the belief system works is not just understanding what it is, but understanding how our mind works. Our belief system works with us on a daily basis to accomplish what we believe and how we handle what we believe. So, let's look at the biology of belief.

The Biology Of Belief- How It Works

Our Soul (psyche) - (Mind) in a human or other conscious being the element, part, substance, or process that reasons, thinks, feels, wills, perceives, judges.

The conscious mind, which represents the seat of our personal identity, source, or spirit—is the creative mind. It can see into the future, review the past, or disconnect from the present moment as it solves problems in our head. In its creative capacity, the "conscious mind holds our wishes, desires, and aspirations for our lives. It is the mind that conjures up our positive thoughts."

The Subconscious- existing or operating in the mind beneath or beyond consciousness: record-playback mechanism, habitual, instincts, experiences, acquires behavior-belief. The subconscious mind is primarily a repository of stimulus-response tapes derived from instincts and learned experiences. The subconscious mind is fundamentally habitual; it will play the same behavioral responses to life's signals over and over again, much to our chagrin. How many times have you found yourself going ballistic over something trivial like an open cereal box? It's because you have been trained since childhood to carefully close it.

The biology of belief is the way that your mind is made to help you think, to ration, to make decisions, and to navigate through life.

So, you can see that it is important to know how your thoughts work, so you will be able to trust God in trouble times.

Let me give you an example of how all of this works.

Your mind has two components - conscious mind- when you are awake in your awaken state and a subconscious mind- your belief system sealed with information from the duration of your life. All of your life you have been storing information in your subconscious. I like to call it the warehouse of your mind. This is the place where everything you allowed to enter your thoughts is stored. Picture it this way. Picture an 18-wheeler truck pulling up to a warehouse and unloading groceries off of the truck into the warehouse. The workers would unpack the truck and load the warehouse. So it is with your mindset that your subconscious mind has been storing information.

Let me explain, you have what is called willpower. You have been given a free will. You can choose to live your life the way you want as long as you don't break the law. You can leave when you want, you can eat what you want, you can go where you want, you can wake up when you want, and you can put on whatever clothes you want and choose whatever style you want to wear your hair. You have a free will to make choices.

Your will, which are your decisions, your likes, your wants, and your choices, is the gate keeper of information.

Now picture this. How does information enter my subconscious mind?

Whatever you read through your eye gate and whatever you hear through your ear gate goes through the door of your conscious mind into the warehouse of your subconscious mind, and it's stored there for future use.

There is a saying that I started the chapter with, and that is 'until you make your subconscious your conscious, it will direct your life, and you will call it fate.'

You will begin to believe that you're not in control of your own life, but that things will automatically happen without your control.

Subconscious thoughts will be what govern your life. Remember, 95% of your awakened state is governed by your subconscious thoughts. That means while you are awake and trying to make decisions, those decisions are pulled from the warehouse of your subconscious mind. Have you ever asked yourself why do I continually do the same things over and over again? Yes, because it is how you shaped your subconscious mind to make decisions. If you want to change the things you've been doing, you must change the way you think. Let me give an example of how you can do that:

1.) Information- Get to know the truth and only allow factual true information to enter your thoughts.

2.) Saturation- Fill your mind with truth because truth matters. It is only the truth that has the promise to set you free.

3.) Meditation- Decide to meditate on truth so you can be continuously contemplating over and over until you become one with the way you think.

4.) Demonstration- show a proof by reasoning and evidence that with you as truth can be demonstrated.

5.) Affirmation- Declare positively and be willing to stand by what you now know to be true.

6.) Transformation- That's when the change comes. You've changed or altered completely in your nature, and your form, and in your function. You've had a metamorphosis. You've been trying to figure out what your mind is doing. You don't think the way you used to; nor do you act the way you used to.

Let me repeat them: Information, Saturation, Meditation, Demonstration, Affirmation, and Transformation.

The Blessings of Biblical Belief- The Benefits

This leads me to the third point of belief, and that is the blessing of Biblical belief. You must begin to embrace that the Bible is true. The Bible says in the book of John 8:32 that you will know the truth, and the truth will set you free. Do you see there is a blessing in Biblical belief, and that blessing is freedom? You must embrace and come to grips with your belief in the Bible. Let the Bible be your guidance. Let the word of God, which is given from God, be your final word.

This is important because our belief system is set by the criteria we say, so we determine what we believe, and we determine what we believe to be true.

Let me close this chapter by giving you some words from God's Bible that can help shape your thoughts as it relates to trusting God in trouble times.

The Bible says in the book of Proverbs 12:21 that no actual evil, misfortune, or calamity shall come up on the righteous, but the wicked shall be filled with evil, misfortune, and calamity. Decide to make that true in your life. Say He will not allow evil or calamity to come upon me.

The Bible says the wicked is overthrown through his wrongdoing and calamity, but the consistently righteous has hope and is confident even in death.

By replacing all thoughts with new thoughts and by replacing worldly thoughts with Biblical truth, you have re-established your thoughts that life is not on the shakiness and uncertainties of the world, but on the firm foundation of God's word.

Chapter Five

Turn Maintained

Trusting God In Trouble Times

In this chapter we are going to focus on how to trust God by maintaining our turn to Him. If you are going to trust God in troubled times, as I've previously stated in other chapters, you are going to have to trust His word. Trust that He is a high tower, and you will have to turn from whatever you previously trusted in and turn to Him; and, not just turn to Him, but maintain that turn.

Again, I do not want you to look at this as some grievous yoke that is being put upon your neck. Instead, I want you to understand that these are just simple principles.

Believe what God's word says concerning trusting Him and receiving from Him- that it will be given by grace and not because of grievous toiling.

I have several ways this can be accomplished. Let's take a look at the first way that your turn can be maintained. The first way that you can maintain your turn is to be conscious of the turn.

Conscious of the Turn

What does it mean to be conscious? To be conscious means to be aware of one's own existence, sensations, thoughts, surroundings, and having the mental faculties fully active.

As you can see, to be conscious of the turn you've made from trusting in others, things, and perhaps something else mean that you are conscious - that you are fully aware and that you are mentally engaged of the decision that was made to turn. In essence, what I am telling you is once that right decision to come to God and to trust Him and His word and His timing during these troubled times has been made, then that decision needs to be maintained. This can only be done on your part. This is something that cannot be done for you because no one can think for you.

Let me briefly explain to you how information gets into our subconscious mind. You must always remember that you have a conscious mind that functions in your awakened state and that you have also been given a subconscious mind that houses information. The information that your subconscious mind houses was given permission by you to enter. How is this, you ask? You have been given five senses: the sense of taste, the sense of touch, the sense of smell, the sense of sight, and the sense of hearing. These senses served as a guard; or, you can say a gatekeeper. There are several ways information enters our mind, either by our sense of sight, we read it, or by our sense of hearing, we heard it.

Your will allows the information to enter in. This information was given permission by you to be stored in your subconscious mind, and anything that is allowed to reside in your subconscious mind will be used 95% of your awakened state.

This means that without even thinking about it, you will automatically go on autopilot.

Let me give you an example. Do you remember when you were learning how to drive? You had to put one hand at 12 o'clock and maybe the other hand at 3 o'clock. You had to focus on the road, and you couldn't do anything else. All you could focus on was getting it right. You didn't want to kill anybody, especially yourself, so you focused on what needed to be done until you learned how to drive. Once you learned how to drive, you have been driving for years now. When you get in your car, you go through the drive through and pick up a hamburger and fries and whatever drink you like. You take off and while driving, you're talking on your cell phone and eating your meal...all while driving. How is this accomplished? How can you now multitask with something that at first was unimaginable? I will tell you how. You allowed the instructions on how to drive to pass your conscious mind and to be stored into your subconscious mind and because 95% of your awakened state is governed by the information in your subconscious mind, you already have the information to know how to drive. It is the same way to make sure that the information that you have allowed to enter your subconscious mind through your conscious mind is the information that solidifies and confirms God's truth.

Once that information has been stored in your subconscious mind through your conscious mind, then when you are not even thinking about it, when you are just going through the course of your regular day, you will begin to make decisions and operate and navigate everyday life knowing that

without even thinking about it, you have to
maintain your turn. That is your trust in God.

Let me give you an example of this in the Bible.
The Bible says in John 14:1.

Let not your heart be troubled: ye believe in God,
believe also in me.

John 14:1 (King James Bible)

I want you to notice that it says let not your heart
be troubled. Remember, we are talking about
ultimately trusting God in trouble times. So, how
do you trust God in times of trouble? How do you
know that God will be there for you? These are the
questions and more that perhaps you've been
asking yourself. That's why in this chapter, and

particularly with this point we're dealing with, turn maintained. And as I previously stated, your will serves as a gatekeeper for information that enters your conscious mind and is stored in your subconscious mind. God verifies this by saying in John 14:1 to let not your heart be troubled. For Him to say this particularly in this way is to say that you have a choice if you would allow your heart to be troubled or not.

Stay with me because I can hear the wheels of your thoughts going round and round; but, you have to understand. To look at the word 'let' means that there is a choice. The thing that the average person does not realize is that we truly have a choice when it comes to matters of the heart.

Trusting God In Trouble Times

Just because there is trouble in the land does not mean that you need to allow that trouble to trouble you. In the amplified version of that text it says do not let your heart be troubled. The amplified version of this text starts with a command of what Jesus would like to see you do.

He's talking to His disciples because He is about to go back to His Father, and He knew that once this happened, His disciples would be troubled. He gives them a command, if you would, in controlling their emotions in the midst of trouble, and that is to not let your heart be troubled. Don't allow trouble to simply walk past your will and to enter your conscious and subconscious mind. Tell the gatekeeper, which is your will, that if it sees trouble don't answer the door. Don't answer the phone. Don't let it pass. Reject it and send it back to where it came from because, ultimately, the choice is yours.

This is why I have previously stated in this book that you must be a partner with God in the success of your life. You cannot idly sit by on the sideline of your life expecting God to do it all. He has already done everything He will ever do, and because of His love for you, He instructs you on what you need to do to receive the answers to life's problems. Remember when I told you in Chapter 1 that truth matters? This is why - because the truth is a choice to either receive trouble or to reject trouble.

I don't know about you, but I am leaping for joy for the fact that I have been given some control over my emotions. Now in order to maintain that turn, let us now look at our second point, and that is how to be consistent in the turn. Not only must I be conscious of the decisions I've made to turn it all over to Him and to lock in that decision, but now I must learn how to stay consistent with everything that was done to make the turn. What does it mean to be consistent?

Consistent in the Turn

To be consistent means to constantly adhere to the same principles, course, or form. It means holding firmly together or coherent. In a nutshell, it means whatever it took for you to get there, keep doing it

to stay there.

Let's take a look at II Corinthians 5:7-12.

(For we walk by faith, not by sight:) We are
confident, *I say,* and willing rather to be absent
from the body, and to be present with the
Lord. Wherefore we labour, that, whether present
or absent, we may be accepted of him. For we
must all appear before the judgment seat of Christ;
that every one may receive the things *done* in *his*
body, according to that he hath done, whether *it be*
good or bad. Knowing therefore the terror of the
Lord, we persuade men; but we are made manifest
unto God; and I trust also are made manifest in
your consciences. For we commend not ourselves
again unto you, but give you occasion to glory on
our behalf, that ye may have somewhat to *answer*
them which glory in appearance, and not in heart.

II Corinthians 5:7-12 (King James Bible)

Notice it says for we walk by faith and not by

sight. That is an important phrase because if you're

going to be consistent in the things of God, it is

going to happen in and through your faith. You learned that your senses were given to you by God for your body to function properly on the earth and not to lead you or your spirit.

He has given you faith to govern and guide your life. That's why Paul can say in Chapter 7 for we walk by faith and not by sight.

Let's look at it in the amplified version. It says for we walk by faith. We regulate our lives and conduct ourselves by our conviction or belief respecting man's relationship to God and divine things with trust and holy fervor, thus we walk not by sight or appearance.

There can be no consistency without God's word once your mind has been filled with the word of

God, and it has nuzzled down in the deep recesses of your subconscious mind.

Do you have yourself set up to be consistent in the things of God? Always remember that this consistency is the key to the breakthrough. If there is going to be any lasting breakthroughs in your life, consistency is the key.

Let's look at our final point now that we have looked at conscious and consistency; we must now look at being committed to the turn.

Committed to the Turn

What does it mean to be committed? To be committed means to be bound or obligated to a person or thing, as by pledge each or assurance. It means to be devoted. If consistency is the key to the breakthrough, then the real question becomes

how committed are you in being consistent in your

turn and conscious of your turn in order to

maintain your turn? I am asking you now in the

middle of all of the trouble and the crisis and

calamities that you are facing right now to stay

conscious. Stay consistent and make a

commitment to do the things necessary to assure

your success. I want to encourage you that it will

not always be the way it is now. Right now we are

faced with the COVID 19 coronavirus. The

government has extended the stay-at-home order

until at least May 15. Life is full of uncertainties.

There seems to be no guarantee in the near future.

You have been quarantined at home for weeks

now. But even in the midst of all of these

problems, there is a light at the end of the tunnel and a silver lining in every cloud.

All I am asking you to do is to stay committed to God because I can assure you He is committed to you. He will not rest until this matter has been fixed. Trust God, beloved. Don't let the problems you're facing cause you to do anything radical. Stay committed to His word. Stay committed to doing those things that His word says should be done, and you will literally watch all of this turn in your favor.

Chapter Six

Talk Master

In this chapter I will show you how to become a talk master. When I say talk master, I am talking about mastering the words that come out of your mouth. The previous chapters have taught you how to make sure that your thoughts are pure and holy and filled with the word of God. Remember in the last chapter that we covered how to maintain a turn from trusting in anything other than God, and part of that was being conscious, consistent, and committed to that turn. Now it's safe to say at this point, you have already checked the subconscious of your mind to make sure that the information that is stored there is Biblical. The Bible tells us what comes out of a man's mouth was first found in his heart. Jesus said that out of the abundance of a man's heart, his mouth speaks.

This proves the point that if you have a pure heart, you will speak pure words. Having said this, let us look at how to become a talk master. The first thing that I would like to look at that is necessary to becoming a talk master is how you must master your will.

Master Your Will

What is your will, and how does it function? I told you in previous chapters that your will is like a security guard. It guards your heart and your mind. It's like a gatekeeper standing on guard securing the gate. The will has been shaped and formed and given this authority by you. Your will is self-control and human desires.

Trusting God In Trouble Times

Let me give you some Biblical stories to help explain how your will functions and just how powerful your will is. Luke 1:26-38 tells the story about Mary, the mother of Jesus.

And in the sixth month the angel Gabriel was sent from God unto a city of Galilee, named Nazareth, To a virgin espoused to a man whose name was Joseph, of the house of David; and the virgin's name *was* Mary. And the angel came in unto her, and said, Hail, *thou that art* highly favoured, the Lord *is* with thee: blessed *art* thou among women. And when she saw *him,* she was troubled at his saying, and cast in her mind what manner of salutation this should be. And the angel said unto her, Fear not, Mary: for thou hast found favour with God. And, behold, thou shalt conceive in thy womb, and bring forth a son, and shalt call his name JESUS. He shall be great, and shall be called the Son of the Highest: and the Lord God shall give unto him the throne of his father David: And he shall reign over the house of Jacob forever; and of his kingdom there shall be no end. Then said Mary unto the angel, How shall this be, seeing I know not a man? And the angel answered and said unto her, The Holy Ghost shall come upon thee, and the power of the Highest shall overshadow thee: therefore also that holy thing which shall be born of thee shall be called the Son of God. And, behold, thy cousin Elisabeth, she hath also conceived a son in her old age: and this is the sixth month with her, who was called barren. For with God nothing shall be impossible. And Mary said, Behold the handmaid of the Lord; be it unto me according to thy word. And the angel departed from her.

Luke 1:26-38 (King James Bible)

What an awesome story about the birth of our Lord and Savior Jesus Christ. I want you to pay close attention to what it says in verse 38. Mary asks a very interesting question to the angel Gabriel. Listen to what Mary said. Mary said, "behold I am the handmaid of the Lord. Let it be done to me according to what you have said." The angel then left. Why is this important, you ask? Because it shows that even though it was God's will and

God's desire for Mary to birth our Savior into this world, God did not just impregnate Mary with Jesus, but He sent His angel Gabriel to ask Mary for permission to use her body. Wow! Did you get that? We are talking about a God who spoke to the waters. He spoke to the sun, the moon, and the stars and created a world that we're living in. We are talking about a God who is all powerful and all-knowing who can do what He wants to do whenever He wants to do it; but, yet, He doesn't violate what I call your will.

I really need you to get this because most people believe that they are powerless, that somehow things out of their control will just happen because this invisible God is a bully, and He goes around invoking His will. That could not be further from the truth. You see, I want to paint a beautiful portrait of a God who you may not know.

This God is so loving and so kind that He desires to have a personal relationship with you unforced. It is not His desire to make you do anything. He will never violate your will. Yes, He created you, and, yes, He has the power to do whatever He wants to. Yet, He will never make you do what you don't want to do. He will never force Himself on you because this is what I call rape.

Whenever a person's will has been violated, you have just committed a crime. That's why God sent Gabriel down to Mary to let her know what His intentions were. God had a plan in His mind to redeem man, and in order for that plan to come to

pass, He needed the participation of a woman.

Remember in Genesis 3:15, God said to the devil

after the fall of Adam and Eve that I will put

enmity between you and the woman and between

your offspring and her offspring. He will bruise

and tread your head underfoot, and you will lie in

wait and bruise His heel.

That was the first prophetic mentioning of the birth

of Jesus Christ.

Gabriel now shows up in the book of Luke 1:26. In

the sixth month, the angel Gabriel was sent from

God to a town of Galilee named Nazareth to a girl

never having been married, and a virgin, engaged

to be married to a man whose name was Joseph, a

descendent of the house of David. The virgin's name was Mary. Remember in verse 38 of that chapter, Mary gave permission to God through Gabriel to use her body as a vessel so that Jesus could be born. This is the same way it works with you, beloved. God will never violate your will. You must give Him permission to use any aspect of your life.

Let us now look at one of the most important stories in history, and that is the story of Jesus in the garden of Gethsemane before His arrest. I want you to take a very close look at His struggles with His will. Yes, Jesus had a free will to do what He wanted to do, but let's look at how He handled the biggest struggle of His earthly life. The Bible tells

of this story in Luke 22:39-46.

And he came out, and went, as he was wont, to the mount of Olives; and his disciples also followed him. And when he was at the place, he said unto them, Pray that ye enter not into temptation. And he was withdrawn from them about a stone's cast, and kneeled down, and prayed, Saying, Father, if thou be willing, remove this cup from me: nevertheless not my will, but thine, be done. And there appeared an angel unto him from heaven, strengthening him. And being in an agony he prayed more earnestly: and his sweat was as it were great drops of blood falling down to the ground. And when he rose up from prayer, and was come to his disciples, he found them sleeping for sorrow, And said unto them, Why sleep ye? rise and pray, lest ye enter into temptation.

Luke 22:39-46 (King James Bible)

In this story, Jesus is found in a place called

Gethsemane. Gethsemane means winepress. It

describes how wine is made. You take grapes, put

them in a barrel, and then you step on them and smash them in order to get the juices extracted from the grapes. There is a smashing process. So here, Jesus is in this place of smashing.

When Jesus was sent to earth by His Heavenly Father, it was understood that God's desire and God's plan to redeem mankind would take place by the willing participation of Jesus Christ giving up His body and His blood as a ransom in order to save the world. This agreement was made in Heaven, and now Jesus finds Himself at the time of fulfilling the previously agreed-upon desire and will of the Father. This can only be accomplished as long as Jesus completes His mission. So here He is praying to God and thinking about all of the things that were about to happen to Him. He thought about the nails that were going to be driven into His wrists. He thought about the nails that were going to be driven into His feet. He thought about the thorns that were going to be smashed upon His head. He thought about the spear that was going to be thrust into His side. He thought about the beating that He was about to take, and He asked the Father if it be Your will let this cup pass from Me. He is now literally asking God the Father is there any other way that We can accomplish redeeming man.

But I want you to pay close attention to His very next statement. He said, nevertheless, not My will but Thy will be done.

You can say that in that very moment with all of the doubt that was running through Jesus's head and all of the concerns that He had. The fact that His human nature kicked in should comfort you in knowing that if Jesus, your Lord and Savior, got to a point where He wanted to change His mind, what about you?

But He demonstrated that even though trouble is mounting up against you and calamities are calling from every side, you are still in control of your will. Decide today that God can have your will. That you will work hand-in-hand fulfilling His desire because, ultimately, you are the master of your own will.

Let's look at becoming a talk master. Not only must you master your will, but you must also master your words. I think it is important for you to understand that words are simply containers for your thoughts. Again, that's why as previously mentioned, your thoughts are extremely important because they enter the atmosphere through your words. Never underestimate the power of your words. Your words are literally the construction company of your life. It shapes your world. It expresses your thoughts. It tells the listener where your head is.

Master Your Words

Let's take a look at the book of Proverbs 18:20-21.

There you will discover just how important

mastering your words is to your life.

A man's belly shall be satisfied with the fruit of his mouth; *and* with the increase of his lips shall he be filled. Death and life *are* in the power of the tongue: and they that love it shall eat the fruit thereof.

Proverbs 18:20-21 (King James Bible)

Listen to how it reads in the amplified version of

Proverbs 18. It says a man's moral self shall be

filled with the fruit of his mouth; and with the

consequence of his words he must be satisfied

whether good or evil. If you think that is

something, listen to what it says in verse 21. Death and life are in the power of the tongue, and they who indulge in it shall eat the fruit of it for death or life.

I know that you can see the seriousness of mastering your words. People tend to think that they can just say anything with no consequences, but that is not true. Every single time we open up our mouths, we need to make sure that we are not saying only what we see, but we are saying what we desire to see. I often tell people to speak it, speak it, speak it until you see it, see it, see it! Why is this important, you ask? Because you've just read in the Scriptures that your life is built upon the words that come out of your mouth. Now you can see an example of this by looking at Genesis 1:1. It speaks of how God created the world. He did not use hammer and nail but simply spoke this world into existence.

If you look at Hebrews 11:1, it confirms this by saying the world that we see was created out of the things that we cannot see. What are those things? Those things are God's word. You are literally creating your life and the world around you with the words that proceed out of your mouth.

Do you now understand the importance of not just blurting anything out of your mouth because of how you feel? Never let your feelings dictate your speaking. Decide today to renovate your life by saying what you desire to see and not just say what you see. By you becoming a talk master by

mastering your words, you are telling all of the

negativity around you that they cannot control

your mouth. Your mouth has found another

master, and that master is Jesus. You will

continually praise Him with the words of your

mouth. Let me list several Scriptures that will

show you the severity and seriousness of mastering

your words.

Let the words of my mouth, and the meditation of
my heart, be acceptable in thy sight, O LORD, my
strength, and my redeemer.

Psalm 19:14 (King James Bible)

The entrance of thy words giveth light; it giveth
understanding unto the simple.

Psalm 119:130 (King James Bible)

A soft answer turneth away wrath: but grievous

words stir up anger.

Proverb 15:1 (King James Bible)

Pleasant words *are as* an honeycomb, sweet to the soul, and health to the bones.

Proverbs 16:24 (King James Bible)

Hopefully the Scriptures previously mentioned

will help secure your thoughts and your mind as it

relates to the power of your words. Mastering your

words simply means being careful not just to say

what comes to your mind but to make sure that

what is in your mind is approved by you because

words matter. Now let's look at the final way that

you can become a talk master and that is to master

your worship.

Master Your Worship

I know that you're thinking do you really expect me to find the strength in the midst of all this trouble and all of these calamities to worship God? By now I would hope that you have had a mind renewal to the fact that God is not responsible for COVID 19 or any other pandemic tragedies that life may throw at you. He is a loving Father, and the Bible says in the book of James that God is a good God and that every good and perfect gift comes from Him. It is His only desire to see you blessed and enjoying the life He's prepared for you.

Let me share with you a portion of my book "Faith to Stay Calm in a Crisis." In this book I have a chapter called Canticle Continually. Decide to

sing songs of praise to God always - no matter

what is going on in your life.

Let's read what the Bible says about temptation

and trouble in the book of James to get a good idea

if God uses problems or trouble to cause us grief or

worse or to train or teach us lessons.

Let no man say when he is tempted, I am tempted
of God: for God cannot be tempted with evil,
neither tempteth he any man: But every man is
tempted, when he is drawn away of his own lust,
and enticed. Then when lust hath conceived, it
bringeth forth sin: and sin, when it is finished,
bringeth forth death. Do not err, my beloved
brethren. Every good gift and every perfect gift is
from above, and cometh down from the Father of
lights, with whom is no variableness, neither
shadow of turning.

James 1:13-17 (King James Bible)

Notice the Bible says in the book of James 1:13, "let no man say when he is tempted that he is tempted of God." God cannot be tempted with evil, neither tempted He any man. Did you hear that? God cannot be tempted with, nor will He tempt any man with evil.

So, it is clear beloved, trouble, grief, and all of those things do not and cannot come from God. God is not a liar. When He says something, He means it. All of the problems, trials, tribulations, and the pain that you are experiencing - it is not God. It is always easy when things are not going right, and when a crisis arises in our lives, or when it seems like we are in a valley experience, to look outwardly to find who is to blame. But, I can assure you as the Scriptures just pointed out, God cannot tempt you. Whenever you're being tempted, it is to cause you to fail. That's why God is not tempting you. God will test you, but never will He tempt you. Test comes to show you where you are in the process. Temptation comes to make you fail or fall. There is no good in temptation.

The Scriptures go on to say that whenever lust is conceived, it brings forth sin and death. I'm not saying that you are to blame for what is going wrong in your life right now. I'm trying to show you that it's not God who is the cause of these problems. I think it's easy for us to point the finger at Him when things are not going well in our lives, but if we study the Scriptures and get a better understanding of who God really is, we will discover that He's not in the temping business.

I really want you to focus on verse 17. It says that every good and perfect gift comes from God. It then stands to reason that He's not the one that causes bad things to happen in our lives.

Let us look at some of the names of God to see if He has a name that means trial, trouble, grief, or pain.

God- Who He Is to Us

- Jehovah/Yahweh- I am who I am
- Jehovah Jireh- the Lord will provide (Ge. 22:14)
- Jehovah Nissi- The lord is my banner (Ex. 17:15)
- Jehovah Shalom- The Lord is peace (Judg. 6:24)

- Jehovah Shammah- The Lord is there (Ezek. 48:35)
- Jehovah Tsebaoth- The Lord of host (I Sam. 1:3)

I want you to notice that every one of these names mean something about His character. He is a good God and worthy of all the praise and worship we could ever give Him.

There are several reasons for troubles and problems to arise in our lives. These can be but are not limited to the following:

A.) **Human Era**- sometimes we make mistakes

B.) **Satanic Attack**- the devil is attacking

C.) **Natural Causes**- Things wear out or just don't work

Trusting God In Trouble Times

The point is, God's heart toward you is for your good only. He is never trying to hurt you. If it was His desire to hurt, He would have never sent His only son to die a gruesome death in order to save you.

Let us now move on to why I believe even in the midst of this season of trouble you're going through that you can still trust God in trouble times, and find it in your heart to talk of His goodness.

The Purpose Of Praise

I will give to the Lord the thanks due to His rightness and justice, and I will sing praise to the name of the Lord Most High.

Psalm 7:17 (Amplified Bible)

The purpose of praise is to tell God how good He is, and to lavish upon Him all of the worship we can give Him. It is important to understand that He is worth all of the glory and the praise that you can give Him. Praise is to value the object of your worship.

The Bible says in the book of Psalms 7:17 I will give to the Lord thanks due to His rightness and justice, and I will sing praise to the name of the Lord Most High.

The psalmist has decided thanking God is worth it. As I previously stated, God will never tempt you. He is not the cause of problems; therefore, He is worthy to be praised. No matter where life finds you, and no matter what's going on in your life, I want you to focus on the goodness of our God.

It is only then that you will be able to praise a God that you see worth in, and you will come to a place where you can trust Him in times of trouble.

Listen to what the Bible says in Psalm 9:1-2

I WILL praise You, O Lord, with my whole heart; I will show forth (recount and tell aloud) all Your marvelous works and wonderful deeds! I will rejoice in You and be in high spirits; I will sing praise to Your name, O Most High!

Psalm 9:1-2 (Amplified Bible)

Notice the psalmist says in verse 2 that he will rejoice in high spirit. He says this because despite all of the things going wrong in his life, he realizes that he would be nothing without God on his side.

He knows that life would be nothing without God. God is the very breath of his existence.

You must develop a mentality that you are going to praise God no matter what. I'm not asking you to forget about what's going on in your life, nor am I suggesting that it doesn't hurt; but, what I am saying is, don't focus on who's to blame or trying to find out whose fault it is.

Remember the goodness of God and praise Him in it - not for it.

In everything give thanks: for this is the will of God in Christ Jesus concerning you.

I Thessalonians 5:18 (King James Bible)

The purpose of praise is to see the worth of the object of your praise and to develop a proper perspective about the problems. This crisis is not

the end of you. He will not allow it to crush you or

destroy you. Find the strength to open your mouth,

lift up your hands, and tell a good God that you

love Him. Tell Him that you honor Him and that

you trust Him with your heart and the troubles. Let

Him bring a calm into your spirit that will allow

you to bare it.

The Participants of Praise

Through Him, therefore, let us constantly and at all
times offer up to God a sacrifice of praise, which is
the fruit of lips that thankfully acknowledge and
confess and glorify His name.

Hebrews 13:15 (Amplified Bible)

Notice it says that we will constantly and

continually offer up to God a sacrifice of praise.

Praising God can sometimes be a sacrifice. We don't always feel like praising God when we're tired, sad, or upset. That's why it's called a sacrifice of praise. We can't sit on the sidelines of life hoping that others will do for us what we need to do for ourselves. Praising God is one of those things we must do for ourselves. You must participate in praising God.

Psalm 150:6 says, "Let everything that hath breath praise the LORD. Praise ye the LORD."

Being an active participant in praising God is good for your soul and your health because it takes your mind and thoughts off of the negatives and focuses on the positives. It causes you to think of the goodness of God and all He's done for you. It literally makes God big and your problems

smaller. Decide today that you are going to praise

Him no matter what and do it.

The Power Of Praise

I WILL bless the Lord at all times; His praise shall
continually be in my mouth. My life makes its
boast in the Lord; let the humble and afflicted hear
and be glad. O magnify the Lord with me, and let
us exalt His name together. I sought (inquired of)
the Lord and required Him [*of necessity and on the
authority of His Word*], and He heard me, and
delivered me from all my fears. They looked to
Him and were radiant; their faces shall never blush
for shame or be confused. This poor man cried,
and the Lord heard him, and saved him out of all
his troubles. The Angel of the Lord encamps
around those who fear Him [*who revere and
worship Him with awe*] and each of them He
delivers. O taste and see that the Lord [*our God*] is
good! Blessed (happy, fortunate, to be envied) is
the man who trusts and takes refuge in Him. O fear
the Lord, you His saints [*revere and worship
Him*]! For there is no want to those who truly
revere and worship Him with godly fear

Psalm 34:1-9 (Amplified Bible)

Praising God has the power to transform your thinking and to elevate you thoughts. It will cause you to see things differently. You will see God in a better light than you previously viewed Him. You see, praise is a heart changer. It fills your heart with gratitude, not despair. David realized how good God has been to him and Israel. He then asked the people to acknowledge the goodness of God by tasting and seeing that He is good.

David says, "For there is no want to those who truly revere and worship Him with godly fear." Worshiping God has the power to meet your needs without you even asking. God knows everything you need, and He's always ready to meet those needs. He knows the trouble you find yourself in right now.

Remember, He's working all things together for your good. That means the good and the bad. Never treat God bad in the middle of a bad situation before you see the end of the thing.

He's causing even the bad to work out for your good. Give it and Him time to work, and you will see that He's for you and not against you. In the meanwhile, decide to praise and worship Him right there in the trouble times. You will see that God was right there with you during your trouble times, and His plans for you are good.

Chapter Seven

Transfer Minded

The proof of trust is the transfer of weight. Always remember this. It is easy to say that you trust God, but the proof that you really trust God is in transferring the weight. I am literally telling you to be transfer minded, and not just transfer minded, but mindful of what you are actually transferring. Let's look at the first point that I would like to make and that is transfer the weight.

Transfer The Weight

Let me tell you of a personal story. Allow me to be transparent for a moment. In 2013 my son Zachary Isaac Antoine was diagnosed with liver cancer. My wife and I had plans to celebrate his one-year-old birthday. We were taking him to his one-year doctor's appointment and after that, we were going to go to the park, roll him around in his stroller, play with him, and just enjoy each other. Unbeknownst to us, this day would change our lives forever. The doctor discovered that my son had a mass on his liver and strongly encouraged us to go straight to the hospital. After the doctors ran all of the tests needed to confirm our worst nightmare, we were informed that, in fact, he did have cancer.

I remember as we battled for weeks and months through the chemotherapy process, one night while my son was asleep in his hospital bed, I sat down on the sofa/bed next to his crib and began to worry and to think about how I was going to handle not just the problems I was facing in that moment, but the weeks ahead. You see, I consider myself a planner and a goal setter. So if I'm going to be faced with having to deal with something, I like to plan ahead. The problem in this situation was that I was not walking in faith - that is trusting God for a favorable outcome. Instead, I discovered that I was walking in fear, worry, stress, and anxiety. I say that because of the statement I started this chapter with and that is the proof of trust is in the transferring of the weight. I pondered over and over in my mind ways that I could deal with this cancer my son had. I continued to think about the diagnosis given to me from the doctors. I went days ahead and tried to factor in everything that could possibly go wrong. I thought that I was a man of faith. For you see, I have been pastoring

God's church for 30 years now. I have taught

people how to trust God. I knew the Scriptures

where it says in Proverbs 3, "Trust in the Lord

with all thine heart; and lean not unto thine own

understanding, but in all thy ways acknowledge

Him and He will direct your path." No one could

tell me that I wasn't a man of faith leaning and

trusting in God. For certain I knew I was walking

in faith.

But wait one moment, let us look at that statement

again - the proof of trusting God is in the transferal

of the weight. We need to go a little deeper with

what I am talking about when I say the transferal

of the weight. I am saying that trials, trouble, and

tribulations carry with them a weight - you can

even say a burden. It is heavy and difficult to carry. It creates stress in your body. One day all of these things - stress, fear, worry, anxiety - were rolling around in my head. One day I felt as if I could have a heart attack because of the cramping, the gas was causing problems. I went to my doctor to be examined and unbeknownst to me, this is what the diagnosis was, she told me that because of all of the stress that I was dealing with, and because of the battle my son was involved in that I had developed gas, and stress was causing my body to react in that way. There it is. I thought that I did what the Bible says in Psalms 55:22 and that is cast thy burden upon the Lord, and He shall sustain and He shall never suffer the righteous to be moved.

Trusting God In Trouble Times

Cast thy burden upon the LORD, and he shall sustain thee: he shall never suffer the righteous to be moved.

Psalm 55:22 (King James Bible)

I thought that I gave the weight of my problems to the Lord; but, in actuality, I was carrying the weight of not just my son's diagnosis but everything else that was going on in my life. You see the proof of trusting God is in transferring the weight from you to Him. It is easy to think that you casted the weight of your cares upon Him, but the proof will manifest itself in your physical body.

This is the test that I want you to take. Let me ask you a few questions so that we can establish who is really carrying the weight. Is there any reaction from your body like cramps, feeling like you are having a heart attack, hair loss, migraine headaches, stomach pain, trouble sleeping, trouble staying focused, and, God forbid, sexual impotency? These are signs from your physical body that there is an enemy that has invaded your body. These are evidence that you are carrying a weight that your physical body was not designed to carry. I had to be honest with myself - preacher or no preacher, pastor or no pastor. If I was going to be the best that I could be and to be there for my son, I had to come to grips with the reality of what I wasn't doing and that is I wasn't giving the weight to God. I was carrying the burden of my own problems. It is my prayer and my strong desire that you have answered these questions honestly and truthfully. Now I am not saying that stress and burdens are the only reasons that your body would manifest these reactions, but could it be that it is? That's why it's important to trust God in your times of trouble, and to transfer the weight of it to Him.

Let me give you another example of properly transferring the weight. Picture this: picture a chair next to you. Picture yourself sitting in the chair. The only reason that you sat in the chair was because you trusted that the chair could hold your weight. You had no doubt that by sitting in this chair, perhaps you sat in for years, would hold you. Not once did you ever check the chair before you sat down. You took the weight of your body and plopped it right down in the chair. This is exactly

what God is telling you. He is trying to get you to

trust Him enough that you believe that if you

transfer the weight of all of these issues that you

have been carrying, He is strong enough that He

can handle them. I was told when I was a little boy

in the baptist church I grew up in, New Zion

Missionary Baptist Church, that our God is a

leaning post, and He can handle the weight.

Transfer The War

It came to pass after this also, *that* the children of
Moab, and the children of Ammon, and with them
other beside the Ammonites, came against
Jehoshaphat to battle. Then there came some that
told Jehoshaphat, saying, There cometh a great
multitude against thee from beyond the sea on this
side Syria; and, behold, they *be* in Hazazon- tamar,
which *is* Engedi. And Jehoshaphat feared, and set
himself to seek the LORD, and proclaimed a fast
throughout all Judah. And Judah gathered

themselves together, to ask *help* of the LORD:
even out of all the cities of Judah they came to
seek the LORD. And Jehoshaphat stood in the
congregation of Judah and Jerusalem, in the house
of the LORD, before the new court, And said, O
LORD God of our fathers, *art* not thou God in
heaven? and rulest *not* thou over all the kingdoms
of the heathen? and in thine hand *is there not*
power and might, so that none is able to withstand
thee? *Art* not thou our God, *who* didst drive out the
inhabitants of this land before thy people Israel,
and gavest it to the seed of Abraham thy friend
forever? And they dwelt therein, and have built
thee a sanctuary therein for thy name, saying, If,
when evil cometh upon us, *as* the sword, judgment,
or pestilence, or famine, we stand before this
house, and in thy presence, (for thy name *is* in this
house,) and cry unto thee in our affliction, then
thou wilt hear and help. And now, behold, the
children of Ammon and Moab and mount Seir,
whom thou wouldest not let Israel invade, when
they came out of the land of Egypt, but they turned
from them, and destroyed them not; Behold, *I say,*
how they reward us, to come to cast us out of thy
possession, which thou hast given us to inherit. O
our God, wilt thou not judge them? for we have no
might against this great company that cometh
against us; neither know we what to do: but our
eyes *are* upon thee. And all Judah stood before the
LORD, with their little ones, their wives, and their
children. Then upon Jahaziel the son of Zechariah,

the son of Benaiah, the son of Jeiel, the son of
Mattaniah, a Levite of the sons of Asaph, came the
Spirit of the LORD in the midst of the
congregation; And he said, Hearken ye, all Judah,
and ye inhabitants of Jerusalem, and thou king
Jehoshaphat, Thus saith the LORD unto you, Be
not afraid nor dismayed by reason of this great
multitude; for the battle *is* not yours, but
God's. Tomorrow go ye down against them:
behold, they come up by the cliff of Ziz; and ye
shall find them at the end of the brook, before the
wilderness of Jeruel. Ye shall not *need* to fight in
this *battle:* set yourselves, stand ye *still,* and see
the salvation of the LORD with you, O Judah and
Jerusalem: fear not, nor be dismayed; tomorrow go
out against them: for the LORD *will be* with
you. And Jehoshaphat bowed his head with *his*
face to the ground: and all Judah and the
inhabitants of Jerusalem fell before the LORD,
worshipping the LORD. And the Levites, of the
children of the Kohathites, and of the children of
the Korhites, stood up to praise the LORD God of
Israel with a loud voice on high. And they rose
early in the morning, and went forth into the
wilderness of Tekoa: and as they went forth,
Jehoshaphat stood and said, Hear me, O Judah, and
ye inhabitants of Jerusalem; Believe in the LORD
your God, so shall ye be established; believe his
prophets, so shall ye prosper. And when he had
consulted with the people, he appointed singers
unto the LORD, and that should praise the beauty

of holiness, as they went out before the army, and to say, Praise the LORD; for his mercy *endureth* forever. And when they began to sing and to praise, the LORD set ambushments against the children of Ammon, Moab, and Mount Seir, which were come against Judah; and they were smitten. For the children of Ammon and Moab stood up against the inhabitants of mount Seir, utterly to slay and destroy *them:* and when they had made an end of the inhabitants of Seir, every one helped to destroy another.

II Chronicles 20:1-23 (King James Bible)

This is a beautiful story of Israel when they was

faced with a battle that seems unwinnable.

Jehoshaphat sought the Lord on behalf of Israel

concerning this battle. We can see in II Chronicles

20:1-23 the story. It says in verse 3 that

Jehoshaphat feared and set himself to seek the

Lord. He knew that there was no human way that

he would be able to win a battle against several

armies that mounted up against him. Perhaps there are things that you are facing that seem unsurmountable. Perhaps you are asking the question, "How in the world am I supposed to face all of this alone?" The Bible says that Jehoshaphat feared. It is totally understandable that when faced with an enemy that is much stronger than you, has more resources than you, and has gotten together with the rest of your enemies to come up against you, it can be scary. I want you to notice that in verse 4 and 5, Jehoshaphat did the wise thing, and that is, he sought the Lord.

I want you to seek the Lord about the very things that you are faced with. You don't have to face these problems alone. God is a very present help in

Trusting God In Trouble Times

time of need. He desires that you would come to Him and ask Him for His assistance. He stands readily available and well capable of helping you.

In verse 7, Jehoshaphat begins to remind God of all of the times that God helped Israel. He reminded God of the enemies that God defeated on behalf of Israel. He was putting God in remembrance of His promises and His covenant with the children of Israel.

God is not a man who should lie. Every promise He's ever made He will fulfill. His promise to you is that He is here ready to do for you the same things He did for Israel. He is ready to drive out the hindrances to your life. He is ready to give you the victory in the midst of your trouble.

I want you to pay close attention to verse 15. It says in verse 15, God said to hearken unto His voice. God said to Israel be not afraid or dismayed of this great multitude, for the battle is not yours but God's.

Did you hear that? God reminded Israel that they did not have to fight this battle, but He would fight for them. He is telling you the exact same thing about troubles you are facing are not yours to face alone but He will fight on your behalf.

I love what it says in verse 20. It says they rose early in the morning and went out into the wilderness of Tekoa, and as they went out, Jehoshaphat stood and said, "Hear me, all Judah, and you inhabitants of Jerusalem. Believe in the Lord your God and you shall be established, believe and remain steadfast to His prophets and you shall prosper."

Jehoshaphat got a revelation that God is the answer. He wanted the people of Judah and Jerusalem to come to the knowledge that with God, this battle was already won.

I want you to do the exact same thing that Israel did, and that is, to understand that no matter what you're faced with, no matter who is coming up against you, and no matter where you find yourself in life, this battle is not yours alone. You have a God who is right here with you and for you, and He will fight for you. I know it can be difficult when things seem like they are about to overtake you and you believe that you're going under. I really want you to trust God in these troubled times. Trust that He cannot lie. Trust the promises He is making to you right now.

I want you to take a deep breath, sit back, close your eyes, and I want you to see yourself coming out victorious. I now want you to begin to praise God for the wonderful things He has done in your life.

By doing this beloved, you are transferring the war out of your hands and into His.

Now let's look at our final point and that is transferring the way. We have already looked at how to transfer the weight and the war. Let's now discover how to transfer the way.

Transfer The Way

THE PLANS of the mind and orderly thinking belong to man, but from the Lord comes the [*wise*] answer of the tongue. All the ways of a man are pure in his own eyes, but the Lord weighs the spirits (the thoughts and intents of the heart). **Roll your works upon the Lord** [*commit and trust them wholly to Him; He will cause your thoughts to become agreeable to His will, and*] **so shall your plans be established and succeed.** The Lord has made everything [*to accommodate itself and contribute*] to its own end and His own purpose--even the wicked [*are fitted for their role*] for the day of calamity and evil. Everyone proud and arrogant in heart is disgusting, hateful, and exceedingly offensive to the Lord; be assured [*I pledge it*] they will not go unpunished. By mercy and love, truth and fidelity [*to God and man--not by sacrificial offerings*], iniquity is purged out of the heart, and by the reverent, worshipful fear of the Lord men depart from and avoid evil. When a man's ways please the Lord, He makes even his enemies to be at peace with him. Better is a little with righteousness (uprightness in every area and relation and right standing with God) than great revenues with injustice. A man's mind plans his way, but **the Lord directs his steps and makes them sure.**

Proverbs 16:1-9 (Amplified Bible)

I absolutely love Proverbs 16. I have come to discover that this text has helped me tremendously in my life. I have learned that no matter what plans I can come up with, it is only the plan of the Lord that will prevail. I have learned to seek the Lord concerning His will and purpose for my life and trust Him that His plans will prevail in my life.

If you are truly going to transfer the way, you will have to learn that the way you take, the way you think, and the way you operate must correspond with Him. When I say way, I'm talking about making plans either to fix or to accomplish some goal or fix some problem. Think of it this way:

whenever you set out on a journey and you're trying to go somewhere, you will map out the way you intend to go - that is the route.

The word way means manner, mode, or fashion, characteristic or habitual manner, a method, plan, or means for attaining a goal, a direction or vicinity, and passage or progress on a course.

As you can see when I say way, I am literally talking about your plans, your process, and your redirection for getting out of the trouble you're in. The Bible says in Proverbs 16:1 the plans of the mind and orderly thinking belongs to man, but from the Lord comes the wise answer of the tongue. All the ways of a man are pure in his own eyes, but the Lord weighs the spirits (the thoughts and intents of the heart).

I particularly love what it says in verse 3, "roll your works upon the Lord (commit and trust them wholly to Him. He will cause your thoughts to become agreeable to His will and) so shall your plans be established and succeed."

Wow! Did you hear that? There is a promise in the word of God that if you would simply give all of your concerns, all of your thoughts, and all of your plans that you have to Him, He will create a way for you where there seems to be no way. He would literally cause your thoughts to become agreeable with His. He would bring your thoughts into synergy with His thoughts, and by doing this, you can literally trust what you're thinking because you now know that your thoughts came from Him. You have the assurance that He is with you during these trouble times, and you can trust Him.

Let me give you some additional Scriptures that will help you to understand the importance of planning.

> **Hear counsel, receive instruction**, and **accept correction**, that you may be wise in the time to come. **Many plans are in a man's mind**, but it is the **Lord's purpose for him that will stand.**
>
> Proverbs 19:20-21 (Amplified Bible)

The word plan means to have in mind as an intention or purpose (a setting forth). When you look at the word plan, I want you to see it as an acronym. (P.L.A.N)

P: Purposeful **L:** Living **A:** Always **N:** Navigates

Always remember that purposeful living always navigates. When you allow your will to become agreeable with His, then your life can be lived on purpose, and that purposeful living will navigate your daily life.

Let me show you by using the acronym I gave you for plan, and combining it with Scriptures, so you can get a better understanding of how God can navigate your daily life through His word and assure you that you can trust Him in trouble times.

I will use each letter in the word plan, and add

Scriptures to help you understand how to trust God

and what His word says concerning trusting Him.

Purposeful Living Always Navigates

P: The Promise When You <u>Pray</u>

MAY THE Lord answer you in the day of trouble!
May the name of the God of Jacob set you up on
high [*and defend you*]; Send you help from the
sanctuary and support, refresh, and strengthen you
from Zion; Remember all your offerings and
accept your burnt sacrifice. Selah [*pause, and think
of that*]! May He grant you according to your
heart's desire and **fulfill all your plans.**

Psalm 20:1-4 (Amplified Bible)

Whenever our hearts in [*tormenting*] **self-
accusation make us feel guilty and condemn us.**
[*For we are in God's hands.*] For He is above and
greater than our consciences (our hearts), and He
knows (perceives and understands) everything
[*nothing is hidden from Him*]. And, beloved, if our
consciences (our hearts) do not accuse us [*if they

do not make us feel guilty and condemn us], we have confidence (complete assurance and boldness) before God, And we receive from Him **whatever we ask**, because we [*watchfully*] obey His orders [*observe His suggestions and injunctions, follow His plan for us*] **and** [*habitually*] **practice what is pleasing to Him.** And this is His order (His command, His injunction): that we should believe in (put our faith and trust in and adhere to and rely on) the name of His Son Jesus Christ (the Messiah), and that we should love one another, just as He has commanded us. All who keep His commandments [*who obey His orders and follow His plan, live and continue to live, to stay and*] abide in Him, and He in them. [*They let Christ be a home to them and they are the home of Christ.*] And by this we know and understand and have the proof that He [*really*] lives and makes His home in us: by the [*Holy*] Spirit Whom He has given us.

I John 3:20-24 (Amplified Bible)

Pray at all times (on every occasion, in every season) in the Spirit, with all [*manner of*] prayer and entreaty. To that end keep alert and watch with strong purpose and perseverance, interceding in behalf of all the saints (God's consecrated people).

Ephesians 6:18 (Amplified Bible)

L: Lean (Trust) In The Lord

MY SON, forget not my law or teaching, but let your heart keep my commandments; For length of days and years of a life [*worth living*] and tranquility [*inward and outward and continuing through old age till death*], these shall they add to you. Let not mercy and kindness [*shutting out all hatred and selfishness*] and truth [*shutting out all deliberate hypocrisy or falsehood*] forsake you; bind them about your neck, write them upon the tablet of your heart. So shall you find favor, good understanding, and high esteem in the sight [*or judgment*] of God and man. **Lean on, trust in, and be confident in the Lord with all your heart and mind** and do not rely on your own insight or understanding. **In all your ways** know, recognize, and acknowledge Him, and **He will direct and make straight and plain your paths.** Be not wise in your own eyes; reverently fear and worship the Lord and turn [*entirely*] away from evil. It shall be health to your nerves and sinews, and marrow and moistening to your bones. Honor the Lord with your capital and sufficiency [*from righteous labors*] and with the first fruits of all your income; So shall your storage places be filled with plenty, and your vats shall be overflowing with new wine.

Proverbs 3:1-10 (Amplified Bible)

We will [*shout in*] triumph at your salvation and victory, and in the name of our God we will set up our banners. May the Lord fulfill all your petitions. Now I know that the Lord saves His anointed; He will answer him from His holy heaven with the saving strength of His right hand. Some trust in and boast of chariots and some of horses, but **we will trust in and boast of the name of the Lord our God.** They are bowed down and fallen, but we are risen and stand upright. O Lord, give victory; let the King answer us when we call.

Psalm 20:5-9 (Amplified Bible)

The Lord brings the counsel of the nations to nought; **He makes the thoughts and plans of the peoples of no effect. The counsel of the Lord stands forever**, the thoughts of His heart through all generations. Blessed (happy, fortunate, to be envied) is the nation whose God is the Lord, the people He has chosen as His heritage. The Lord looks from heaven, He beholds all the sons of men; From His dwelling place He looks [*intently*] upon all the inhabitants of the earth-- He Who fashions the hearts of them all, **Who considers all their doings**. No king is saved by the great size and power of his army; a mighty man is not delivered by [*his*] much strength. A horse is devoid of value for victory; neither does he deliver any by his great power. Behold, the Lord's eye is upon those who fear Him [*who revere and worship Him with awe*], **who wait for Him and hope in His mercy and loving-kindness,** To deliver them from death and keep them alive in famine. Our inner selves wait [*earnestly*] for the Lord; He is our Help and our Shield. For in Him does our heart rejoice, because **we have trusted (relied on and been confident) in His holy name.** Let Your mercy and loving-kindness, O Lord, be upon us, in proportion to our waiting and hoping for You.

Psalm 33:10-22 (Amplified Bible)

Many, O Lord my God, are the wonderful works which You have done, and **Your thoughts toward us**; no one can compare with You! If I should declare and speak of them, they are too many to be numbered. [*As for me*] I am poor and needy, yet the **Lord takes thought and plans for me**. You are my Help and my Deliverer. O my God, do not tarry

Psalm 40:5,17 (Amplified Bible)

He rebuked the Red Sea also, and it dried up; so He led them through the depths as through a pastureland. And He saved them from the hand of him that hated them, and redeemed them from the

hand of the [*Egyptian*] enemy. And the waters
covered their adversaries; not one of them was left.
Then [*Israel*] **believed His words [*trusting in,
relying on them*]**; they sang His praise. But they
hastily forgot His works; they did not [*earnestly*]
wait for His plans [*to develop*] regarding them,

Psalm 106:9-13 (Amplified Bible)

Purposes and plans are established by **counsel**;
and [*only*] with good advice make or carry on war.

Proverbs 20:18 (Amplified Bible)

A: Ask God

Call to Me and I will answer you and show you
great and mighty things, fenced in and hidden,
which you do not know (do not distinguish and
recognize, have knowledge of and understand).

Jeremiah 33:3 (Amplified Bible)

Truly I tell you, whatever you forbid and declare to
be improper and unlawful on earth must be what is
already forbidden in heaven, and whatever you
permit and declare proper and lawful on earth must

be what is already permitted in heaven. Again I tell you, if two of you on earth agree (harmonize together, make a symphony together) about whatever [*anything and everything*] **they may ask,** it will come to pass and be done for them by My Father in heaven.

Matthew 18:18-19 (Amplified Bible)

When the disciples saw it, they marveled greatly and asked, How is it that the fig tree has withered away all at once? And Jesus answered them, Truly I say to you, if you have faith (a firm relying trust) and do not doubt, you will not only do what has been done to the fig tree, but even if you say to this mountain, Be taken up and cast into the sea, it will be done. And **whatever you ask for in prayer**, having faith and [*really*] believing, you will receive.

Matthew 21:20-22 (Amplified Bible)

So I say to you, **Ask and keep on asking** and it shall be given you; seek and keep on seeking and you shall find; knock and keep on knocking and the door shall be opened to you. For everyone who **asks and keeps on asking receives**; and he who seeks and keeps on seeking finds; and to him who knocks and keeps on knocking, the door shall be opened. What father among you, if his son asks for a loaf of bread, will give him a stone; or if he asks for a fish, will instead of a fish give him a serpent? Or if he asks for an egg, will give him a scorpion?If you then, evil as you are, know how to give good gifts [*gifts that are to their advantage*] to your children, how much more will your heavenly Father give the Holy Spirit to those who ask and continue to ask Him!

Luke 11:9-13 (Amplified Bible)

Believe Me that I am in the Father and the Father in Me; or else believe Me for the sake of the [*very*] works themselves. [*If you cannot trust Me, at least let these works that I do in My Father's name convince you.*] I assure you, most solemnly I tell you, if anyone steadfastly believes in Me, he will himself be able to do the things that I do; and he will do even greater things than these, because I go to the Father. And **I will do [*I Myself will grant*] whatever you ask in My Name** [*as presenting all that I AM*], so that the Father may be glorified and extolled in (through) the Son. [**_Yes_**] **I will grant [*I Myself will do for you*] whatever you shall ask in My Name [_as presenting all that I AM_].** If you [*really*] love Me, you will keep (obey) My commands. And I will ask the Father, and He will give you another Comforter (Counselor, Helper,

Intercessor, Advocate, Strengthener, and Standby),
that He may remain with you forever-- The Spirit
of Truth, Whom the world cannot receive
(welcome, take to its heart), because it does not see
Him or know and recognize Him. But you know
and recognize Him, for He lives with you
[*constantly*] and will be in you. I will not leave you
as orphans [*comfortless, desolate, bereaved,
forlorn, helpless*]; I will come [*back*] to you.

John 14:11-18 (Amplified Bible)

N: Nepotism- the act of showing favoritism to
relative or friends in the work place. He favors you

The steps of a [*good*] man are directed and
established by the Lord when He delights in his
way [*and He busies Himself with his every step*].
Though he falls, he shall not be utterly cast down,
for the Lord grasps his hand in support and
upholds him. I have been young and now am old,
yet have I not seen the [*uncompromisingly*]
righteous forsaken or their seed begging bread. All
day long they are merciful and deal graciously;
they lend, and their offspring are blessed.

Psalm 37:23-26 (Amplified Bible)

For those whom He foreknew [*of whom He was aware and loved beforehand*], He also destined from the beginning [*foreordaining them*] to be molded into the image of His Son [*and share inwardly His likeness*], that He might become the firstborn among many brethren. And those whom He thus foreordained, He also called; and those whom He called, He also justified (acquitted, made righteous, putting them into right standing with Himself). And those whom He justified, He also glorified [*raising them to a heavenly dignity and condition or state of being*]. What then shall we say to [*all*] this? If God is for us, who [*can be*] against us? [*Who can be our foe, if God is on our side?*] He who did not withhold or spare [*even*] His own Son but gave Him up for us all, will He not also with Him freely and graciously give us all [*other*] things? Who shall bring any charge against God's elect [*when it is*] God Who justifies [*that is, Who puts us in right relation to Himself? Who shall come forward and accuse or impeach those whom God has chosen? Will God, Who acquits us?*] Who is there to condemn [*us*]? Will Christ Jesus (the Messiah), Who died, or rather Who was raised from the dead, Who is at the right hand of God actually pleading as He intercedes for us? Who shall ever separate us from Christ's love? Shall suffering and affliction and tribulation? Or calamity and distress? Or persecution or hunger or destitution or peril or sword? Even as it is written, For Thy sake we are put to death all the day long;

we are regarded and counted as sheep for the slaughter. Yet amid all these things we are more than conquerors and gain a surpassing victory through Him Who loved us.

Romans 8:29-37 (Amplified Bible)

May grace (God's unmerited favor) and spiritual peace [*which means peace with God and harmony, unity, and undisturbedness*] be yours from God our Father and from the Lord Jesus Christ. May blessing (praise, laudation, and eulogy) be to the God and Father of our Lord Jesus Christ (the Messiah) Who has blessed us in Christ with every spiritual (given by the Holy Spirit) blessing in the heavenly realm! Even as [*in His love*] **He chose us** [*actually picked us out for Himself as His own*] in Christ before the foundation of the world, that we should be holy (consecrated and set apart for Him) and blameless in His sight, even above reproach, before Him in love. For He foreordained us **(destined us, planned in love for us) to be adopted (revealed) as His own children through Jesus Christ,** in accordance with the purpose of His will [*because it pleased Him and was His kind intent*]-- [*So that we might be*] to the praise and the commendation of His glorious grace (favor and mercy), which He so freely bestowed on us in the Beloved. In Him we have redemption (deliverance and salvation) through His blood, the remission (forgiveness) of our offenses (shortcomings and trespasses), in accordance with the riches and the generosity of His gracious favor, Which He lavished upon us in every kind of wisdom and understanding (practical insight and prudence), **Making known to us the mystery (secret) of His will (of His plan, of His purpose).** [*And it is this:*] In accordance with His good pleasure (His merciful intention) which He had previously purposed and set forth in Him. [*He planned*] for the maturity of the times and the climax of the ages to unify all things and head them up and consummate them in Christ, [*both*] things in heaven and things on the earth. In Him we also were made [*God's*] heritage (portion) and we obtained an inheritance; for we had been foreordained (chosen and appointed beforehand) **in accordance with His purpose,** Who works out everything in agreement with **the counsel and design of His [*own*] will**, So that we who first hoped in Christ [*who first put our confidence in Him have been destined and appointed to*] live for the praise of His glory!

Ephesians 1:2-12 (Amplified Bible)

For all who are led by the Spirit of God are **sons of God**. For [*the Spirit which*] you have now received [*is*] not a spirit of slavery to put you once more in bondage to fear, but you have received the **Spirit of adoption [*the Spirit producing sonship*] in [*the bliss of*] which we cry, Abba (Father)! Father!** The Spirit Himself [*thus*] testifies together with our own spirit, **[*assuring us*] that we are children of God**. And if we are [*His*] children, then **we are [*His*] heirs also: heirs of God and fellow heirs with Christ [*sharing His inheritance with Him*]**; only we must share His suffering if we are to share His glory.

Romans 8:14-17 (Amplified Bible)

I have used a lot of Scriptures trying to help you to see that God has made a lot of promises in His word concerning helping you. He is committed to helping you in troubled times. It is my prayer that as you've read through all of the Scriptures that I have previously listed, they would help to comfort you and to help you in the midst of your trouble.

Remember, I took the word plan and used each letter to lay out Scriptures relating to how God intends to assist you. He is there to carry the weight. He is there to fight the war, and He is there to show you the way. I want you to develop such an intimate relationship with God that it becomes second nature to you to trust Him in trouble times.

Chapter Eight

Teachable Mankind

What does it mean to be teachable? It means one

who is able to be taught. It speaks of a person with

the mentality that they don't know it all. It is a

person who's open to learn new information. If you

are going to be a person who can truly trust God in

troubled times, then you will have to remain

teachable.

Let's look in the Bible at the book of

Proverbs 3:1-4.

My son, forget not my law; but let thine heart keep
my commandments: For length of days, and long
life, and peace, shall they add to thee. Let not
mercy and truth forsake thee: bind them about thy
neck; write them upon the table of thine heart: So
shalt thou find favour and good understanding in
the sight of God and man. Trust in the LORD with
all thine heart; and lean not unto thine own
understanding. In all thy ways acknowledge him,
and he shall direct thy paths. Be not wise in thine
own eyes: fear the LORD, and depart from evil. It
shall be health to thy navel, and marrow to thy

bones. Honour the LORD with thy substance, and with the first fruits of all thine increase:

Proverbs 3:1-9 (King James Bible)

Solomon is trying to give his son some wisdom.

He is teaching his son the word of God. Solomon

says to his son in verse 1 not to forget his

teachings. He is encouraging his son to remain

teachable. He is telling him that if he wanted to see

good success and have a long life filled with good

things, that he will have to remain teachable.

It is imperative that as you go through life that you

remain teachable.

Let me give you five traits of a teachable person. I

want you to examine yourself and to see if you

possess these traits. Don't worry. If you don't

possess these traits, then this is easy; you simply can apply them to your life. I want you to read these five traits not as an attempt to put you down, but as my attempt to give you a template by which you can measure where you are as it relates to being or becoming a teachable person.

Five Traits of a Teachable Person

1) Teachable people are thought minded

These are people who have an attitude that's conducive to learning. Their mindset is always and ever obtaining knowledge not just for themselves, but for the benefit of those in their lives. They believe that life moves at the speed of thought. They understand that in order to accomplish any meaningful thing in life, they must be ever learning. They understand that this world is governed by information, and information is growing at the speed of light.

2) Teachable people possess a teachable mindset

These are people who have a strong desire to be taught. They developed the capacity to handle as much information as possible. They realize that 85% of success is due to their attitude, and only 15% is due to their ability. They remind themselves on a consistent and daily basis that they do not know it all. They realize the importance of asking questions because it is in asking questions answers can be found.

3) Teachable people trust mirrors

Let us read what the Bible says in the book of

James 1:22-25,

"But be ye doers of the word, and not hearers only, deceiving your own selves. For if any be a hearer of the word, and not a doer, he is like unto a man beholding his natural face in a glass: For he beholdeth himself, and goeth his way, and straightway forgetteth what manner of man he was. But whoso looketh into the perfect law of liberty, and continueth *therein,* he being not a forgetful hearer, but a doer of the work, this man shall be blessed in his deed.

James 1:22-25 (King James Bible)

It is clear here in the book of James that you

should not just be a person who looks into a mirror

and makes no changes. The purpose of a mirror is

to show you exactly what you look like. The

mirror cannot lie. If there is something out of order

or if there is something undesirable in your appearance, the mirror will reveal it. James is explaining to the readers of the Bible that the word of God is considered a mirror. God's word will reveal the true essence of who we are. He is trying to convey the thought that we should be doers of God's word and not just hearers only.

Remember, a teachable person trusts the mirrors. When a reliable source is endeavoring to give you information, it would behoove you to listen and to remain teachable.

4) Teachable people allow teachable moments

Teachable people will always allow others to speak into their lives. They will cherish what I call teachable moments. These are moments set aside for them to learn from others. These individuals have established relationships with people that they trust with their thoughts. They have developed a relationship that is trustworthy of other teachers being allowed to teach them. They have learned not only to gather information, but to apply the information gathered because they realize that application makes the difference.

5) Teachable people are tactic motivated

These are people who evaluate the methods by which they obtain information. They are motivated by a set of guidelines that they have created in order for such information to improve the quality of their lives. Their tactics are test proven. These people make it a daily habit of learning and obtaining new information every day. It is their daily habit in improving the quality of their life by the method and motivation of the information that is obtained.

Listen to what the Bible says in II Timothy 2:15, "Study to show thyself approved unto God, a workman that needeth not to be ashamed, rightly dividing the word of truth."

Paul is admonishing his son Timothy to study the word of God. He's telling Timothy to remain teachable by the words that he reads from God's Bible. He's reminding Timothy of the importance of trusting God's word as final truth in his life, and to take that word that was taught to him and to teach it to others.

These are five ways that if applied can help you to become a teachable person. The key to applying these principles to your life is to remember that preparation, contemplation, and application can assure that you develop into the best individual that you can be. Applying the information learned because you are teachable; contemplating by asking yourself what have you learned; and, ultimately, applying the learned information to your life by remembering that you're not perfect, and you will make mistakes – but, you will learn from those mistakes, and you will use them to ensure your success.

Chapter Nine

Touch Not Mine

Trusting God In Trouble Times

You can trust God in trouble times because of the promise He made in His word to protect you.

Listen to what God says in 1 Chronicles 16:20-30.

And *when* they went from nation to nation, and from *one* kingdom to another people; He suffered no man to do them wrong: yea, he reproved kings for their sakes, *Saying,* Touch not mine anointed, and do my prophets no harm. Sing unto the LORD, all the earth; shew forth from day to day his salvation. Declare his glory among the heathen; his marvelous works among all nations. For great *is* the LORD, and greatly to be praised: he also *is* to be feared above all gods. For all the gods of the people *are* idols: but the LORD made the heavens. Glory and honour *are* in his presence; strength and gladness *are* in his place. Give unto the LORD, ye kindreds of the people, give unto the LORD glory and strength. Give unto the LORD the glory *due* unto his name: bring an offering, and come before him: worship the LORD in the beauty of holiness. Fear before him, all the earth: the world also shall be stable, that it be not moved.

I Chronicles 16:20-30 (King James Bible)

Trusting God In Trouble Times

What a wonderful song written by David and shared with his people about the wonderful things God has done in the life of David. David would often write songs to commemorate and to remind the readers of the book of Psalms of the goodness of our God, he has come to know in a very personal way. David often found himself with opposition that seems unbeatable. He had to learn how to put his trust in God.

I want you to look at what David says in verse 22. He says touch not Mine anointed, and do My prophets no harm. David is making the declaration that no one could touch him because of the anointing that God has on his life. The enemy could not get a grip on David. It is my prayer that you come to the realization that by trusting God, you too have been put on the do not touch list.

The Untouchables

Let me give you an example from a created insect made by God to teach you how you are truly untouchable. Let's learn a lesson from a spider.

Lessons From a Spider

Spiders are air-breathing arthropods that have eight legs, chelicerae with fangs, able to inject venom, and spinnerets that extrude silk. They are the largest order of arachnids and rank seventh in total species diversity among all orders of organisms.

Spider silk is a protein fiber spun by spiders. Spiders use their silk to make webs or other structures, which function as sticky nets to catch other animals, or as nests, or cocoons to protect

their offspring, or to wrap up prey. They can also

use their silk to suspend themselves, to float

through the air, or to glide away from predators.

Most spiders vary the thickness and stickiness of

their silk for different uses.

In some cases, spiders may even use silk as a

source of food. While methods have been

developed to collect silk from a spider by force, it

is difficult to gather silk from many spiders in a

small space.

Have you ever wondered why is it that a spider can

spin a web that's sticky enough to trap everything

that touches it except the spider? The reason for

this is the spider has an oily like substance on its

little feet that keeps it from sticking to the web. After analyzing several compounds washed off the spiders' legs, researchers found several oily substances — including dodecane, tridecane, and tetradecane — that could act as a non-stick coating.

The same spider that spins the web cannot be trapped by the web.

I'm submitting to you that God has made you oily. He has anointed you with His Holy Spirit. It is the Spirit that makes it impossible for the enemy to get a solid grip on you.

Listen to what the Bible says in 1 John 5:18-21 in the amplified Bible. We know, absolutely, that anyone born of God does not deliberately and knowingly practice committing sin, but the One

Who was begotten of God carefully watches over

and protects him. Christ's divine presence within

him preserves him against the evil, and the wicked

one does not lay hold, get a grip on him, or touch

him. We know positively that we are of God, and

the whole world around us is under the power of

the evil one. And we have seen and know

positively that the son of God has actually come to

this world and has given us understanding and

insight progressively to perceive, recognize, and

come to know better and more clearly Him Who is

true. We are in Him Who is true-in His Son Jesus

Christ, the Messiah. This Man is the true God and

Life eternal. Little children, keep yourselves from

idols and false gods, from anything and everything

that would occupy the place in your heart due to God, from any sort of substitute for Him that would take first place in your life.

I want you to pay close attention to verse 18. It says in the latter clauses of the verse, the evil wicked one does not lay hold or get a grip on him or touch him.

The Bible just told you that your enemy cannot get a grip on you, and the reason they cannot get a grip on you is because you are oily. I want you to let that thought sink in for a minute. Take a deep breath, close your eyes, and imagine that the trials and tribulations that you are going through will not be able to overtake you because you have the presence of the Holy Spirit living on inside of you, which makes you oily. It is the anointing of the Holy Spirit that breaks every yoke and destroys every burden. When I tell you that you are oily, I'm saying that you are just like a spider who will not stick to the web he spins. The enemy will not get a grip or firm hold on you. That's wonderful news! The fact that the enemy cannot get a firm grip or hold on you is absolutely great news.

I want you to repeat after me, and say, I am oily! Repeat it - I am oily! I want you to begin to see yourself as untouchable. Now I am not saying that things won't happen, but what I am saying is, you have an inner protection that makes you oily, and just like the spider, things may come up against you; but, it won't stick to you. The next time you are faced with troubles, I want you to see yourself as a person that is unable to remain in the grips of those troubles.

You have what it takes. You have been bought with a price. You are in the family of God now, and He makes a promise to you that He will always be with you, and He will never leave you alone. The next time you see a spider spinning his web in order to trap his food for that day, I want you to picture yourself not as the spider spinning a web, but as a person who will not stick to anything that has been laid as a trap for you. I want you to envision yourself being able, with God's help, to maneuver through life without the trials and tribulations being stuck to you.

Trusting God In Trouble Times

Whatever you're going through, whatever you are dealing with, you have been anointed not to deal with these problems for the rest of your life. See them falling right off of you and unable to hold you in its grip. Why? Because you are untouchable. You can now put your trust in God during these trouble times, because He's there to help you.

Chapter Ten

Transformation

Manifestation

What do I mean when I say transformation manifestation? I am trying to reveal to you that if you have read this far in this book, and you have applied the principles that I have laid out, there should be a manifested transformation in your life that is so tangible that people can see it. Transformation means to change or alter completely in nature, form, or function. So it stands to reason that the way you handle trouble now has changed. You have literally been transformed in the way you deal with trouble, and that transformation has manifested in your life to the degree where people have noticed the change.

I hear you. You're saying right now, wow. I was just saying that. I was just telling somebody the other day I feel better. Let me congratulate you, but we have a little ways to go. I do celebrate your transformation right there alongside you. Congratulations, you have been transformed into a stronger, wiser, and better person who no longer collapses under the weight of troubles.

There was a saying when I was younger that went:

I'm not where I'm supposed to be. I'm not what I want to be. But, I'm not what I used to be. I haven't learned how to arrive. I've learned how to keep going, and I will be better tomorrow than what I am today, because I have been transformed into a better me. Let me give you another acronym for the word smart, and we will use it as a guideline to help you to continue with your transformation.

Using The S.M.A.R.T Guidelines:

➤ **Specific-** when improving, don't use words like, bigger, or faster. Be specific about your goals.

➤ **Measurable-** your improvement must be measurable. How do you know when you get there and you have truly changed?

➤ **Attainable-** improvement must be something you can actually achieve. Wanting to be a professional boxer at age 85 may not be attainable.

➤ **Realistic-** is the improvement you desire a real goal or too distant? Wanting to run a 50 mile marathon in one week is probably not realistic.

➢ **Timed**- to be held accountable,

improvement must be within a time limit.

Someday is not a real goal.

It is my prayer that by using this acronym
"S.M.A.R.T", it can help you in the future to
remember all of the work you have put in for you
to see the transformation manifestation you are
either enjoying now, or you will enjoy very
shortly.

I want you to take a moment and celebrate all of
the improvements and transformations you have
worked so hard to accomplish. I believe in having
seasons of celebrations and moments set aside to
magnify those improvements. I don't want you to
be so bogged down and goal driven, you forget to

simply celebrate even the smallest victories in your life. I may have never met you, but I want you to picture me on the sideline of your life clapping, rejoicing, with this huge smile on my face as your personal cheerleader. I am so proud of you. I am proud of the person you are becoming.

Remember, Rome was not built overnight, so celebrate! If I were you I would buy a cake, and perhaps some ice cream, balloons, and maybe even a whistle, and I would throw myself the biggest congratulatory celebration that I can muster up, because, beloved, you deserve it.

Let me show you a promise in God's word about how He will bring to pass the petition of your heart and why you are celebrating your transformation

right now. Let's go to the book of Psalms 37:3-5.

Trust in the LORD, and do good; *so* shalt thou
dwell in the land, and verily thou shalt be
fed. Delight thyself also in the LORD; and he shall
give thee the desires of thine heart. Commit thy
way unto the LORD; trust also in him; and he shall
bring *it* to pass.

Psalm 37:3-5 (King James Bible)

The key to these Scriptures is found in verse 5

where it says, "Commit thy way unto the Lord,

trust also in Him, and He shall bring it to pass."

That is exactly what He just did for you. He has

brought your transformation into manifestation.

Don't despise small victories. Don't look down on

yourself or wish you were further along.

Trusting God In Trouble Times

I want you to be grateful for the transformation you have already experienced, and to become hopeful about the manifestation that is still yet to come. I believe going forward you are trusting God in these trouble times. I believe that you have developed a God like boldness. I can see you in my mind's eye, standing there looking your troubles in the eyes, and telling them, God's got me and I got this. Wow, you have become stronger, wiser, and better; and, beloved, I truly celebrate your transformation.

Chapter Eleven

Thrive Magnificently

Trusting God In Trouble Times

In this chapter I will begin to motivate you on something that at first may seem strange, but it is my desire that as you continue to read, your heart will begin to hope and to believe for more out of life and not just to make it. I warn you - what I am about to tell you goes further than just surviving. I am about to encourage you to reach beyond your breaking point and to stretch beyond your realities. I want to motivate you to thrive magnificently. When I say thrive, I am talking about prospering, having good fortune or success, to grow or develop vigorously, and to flourish. As you can see, because you have transformed in the previous chapter, I believe that you're ready to flourish in this chapter. Let's begin.

High Hopes

The attributes of hope:

- ➢ Hope shines brightest in darkness

- ➢ Hope motivates continually

- ➢ Hope energizes you when you're feeling low

- ➢ Hope sweetens the bitter days

- ➢ Hope sings songs of joy and expectation

- ➢ Hope believes all things are possible

- ➢ Hope climbs the highest mountains

- ➢ Hope endures through the hardest times

- ➢ Hope smiles no matter what

- ➢ Hope reaches beyond the breaking points

- ➢ Hopes presses to the end

The attributes of hope are the things you can count on when you have high hopes. It is when you elevate your hope in the things that God has promised, you can then experience all of the attributes that hope has. Hope has its roots in faith, and faith in God never disappoints. I have often heard people make this statement, "don't get your hopes up." But I submit to you that not getting your hopes up can hurt you. It is when your hope is raised that your faith can attach itself to your hope and begin to have high expectations for only good. I believe that it is important that you understand Biblical hope. Biblical hope is to believe and to have high expectations for only good.

Let me give you an example: a person who says I hope I get the job and says it in such a way that they open themselves up for a small percentage of that actually happening is not hoping with Biblical hope. A person who walks in Biblical hope answers the question quite differently. Their response is, "I will get the job" because their hope is not in the chance that they won't get the job but their hope has been elevated in the fact that the job is already theirs.

Let us read in the book of Hebrews 11:1.

Now faith is the substance of things hoped for, the evidence of things not seen.

Hebrews 11:1 (King James Bible)

Notice that the Bible says that faith is the substance of things hoped for. If faith is the substance of things that you are hoping for, then it stands to reason that faith has attached itself to your hopes; and, if your hopes are low, then your faith is also low. If your hopes are high, then your faith is also high. This is important because we receive everything from God through faith. Faith is the foundation by which God deals with us. Faith is being fully persuaded that what God says will happen; so, therefore, high hopes raise the level of your faith, which positions you to receive your heart's desire from a God who cannot lie. Never again make this statement, "I hope so' with a negative connotation. Instead, hope enthusiastically for only good. Hope says yes to life, and it empowers you. Hope can fill you with energy and focus you forward. Hope is a difference maker. Hope looks for a lesson in every defeat, discovers what can be done, regards problems as opportunities, and lights a candle in darkness. Hope views failure as a steppingstone, not a tombstone. Hope tells you that you will make it even in trouble times.

The reason I spent several pages describing hope and explaining it is because helplessness will always lead to hopelessness, and if there is no hope of thriving in the midst of troubles, then there can be no trust in God.

Huge Harvest

Let us close this chapter by looking at a beautiful

story in the Bible found in Genesis 26:1-6, 12-14.

And there was a famine in the land, beside the first
famine that was in the days of Abraham. And Isaac
went unto Abimelech king of the Philistines unto
Gerar. And the LORD appeared unto him, and
said, Go not down into Egypt; dwell in the land
which I shall tell thee of: Sojourn in this land, and
I will be with thee, and will bless thee; for unto
thee, and unto thy seed, I will give all these
countries, and I will perform the oath which I
swear unto Abraham thy father; And I will make
thy seed to multiply as the stars of heaven, and will
give unto thy seed all these countries; and in thy
seed shall all the nations of the earth be
blessed; Because that Abraham obeyed my voice,
and kept my charge, my commandments, my
statutes, and my laws. And Isaac dwelt in Gerar:

Then Isaac sowed in that land, and received in the
same year an hundredfold: and the LORD blessed
him. And the man waxed great, and went forward,
and grew until he became very great: For he had
possession of flocks, and possession of herds, and

great store of servants: and the Philistines envied him.

Genesis 26:1-6, 12-14 (King James Bible)

This is a beautiful story of how God can provide for you in the midst of a crisis and pandemic. Isaac and the children of Israel found themselves in the land of Gerar. Times were so difficult that crops didn't grow, the land was dry, there was a shortage in food supply, and the people decided that they would go into Egypt where they could find food and supplies for their families. Isaac decided that he, too, would go find greener pastures, but God had something else in mind. He instructed Isaac not to go to Egypt but to trust Him for his needs. Can you imagine that there is no food around to feed your family, and no possible way to provide for your family, and then God tells you to stay in the very place that has dried up? I submit to you that God was trying to get Isaac to put his hopes, and his faith in Him, and not in a foreign place for supplies. God knew exactly what He was going to do for Isaac and his family. It was God's plan to always provide for the needs of Isaac, but He needed Isaac to trust Him in trouble times.

So the lesson began, Isaac, I don't want you to go anywhere. Stay right there in the land where I put you and watch Me provide for you. The Bible says that God told Isaac- because Abraham listened to and obeyed His voice and His charge, that He was going to bless Abraham with posterity.

I want you to look very closely at verses 12 to 14. It says, then Isaac sowed a seed and received in the same year 100 times as much as he had planted, and the Lord favored him with blessings. And the man became great and gained more and more until he became very wealthy and distinguished.

The reason that I want you to read Genesis 26 is because there lies the proof that if you can trust God in trouble times, not only will He see you through the trouble times, but He will allow you to thrive magnificently. We serve a God who is not limited by this world's economy. The Bible says that God promises to supply all of your needs according to His riches in glory. Not only were Isaac's needs met, but he prospered in the midst of a famine. While others were simply trying to survive, Isaac was thriving. It is my prayer that your hopes and your faith are so high that you begin to believe that not only will you make it through these trouble times, but that you, too, can thrive magnificently.

Chapter Twelve

Track Record Memories

For whatsoever things were written aforetime were
written for our learning, that we through patience
and comfort of the scriptures might have hope.

Romans 15:4 (King James Bible)

I believe it is important for us to look back over

the track record of our Heavenly Father and to

judge Him based on how He performed in the past.

The Bible says in Romans 15:4 that whatsoever

things were written aforetime were written for our

learning.

The Old Testament was written for you to learn

about Christ. Jesus Christ is concealed in the Old

Testament, but He has been revealed in the New

Testament.

Every story that you read from the book of Genesis

to the book of Malachi depicts how God dealt with

His people in those times. They are filled with story after story, and situation after situation, about how God delivered the Israelites. It was written so that you can have God's resume at your fingertips. Let me caution you about reading the Old Testament and taking everything literally.

God deals with His people in times and seasons. From Genesis to the book of Malachi is considered the Old Testament, and there were different dispensations of how God dealt with Israel. We now live in what is considered the New Testament church, that is, the new covenant. Because of Jesus's finished work on the cross, we have been ushered into the dispensation of grace. When you read how God dealt with the Old Testament saints, be careful not to interject that this is how He will deal with you. I like to tell people to look at it this way.

There are two words that I want you to keep in mind, and they are, description and prescription. It is important to know the difference when you're reading the Bible. When you read a story in the Bible, make sure that you understand if God is describing how He handled that situation versus if He is prescribing how IIc's going to help you.

I believe many times we read stories in the Bible and we mimic what was being done at that time. Always remember that God promises to deliver you, but how He does it is up to Him. I believe God has over 1 billion ways to deliver you, so you don't have to expect Him to move like He moved in the past. When you read the Old Testament, it is to build your hope in a God whose track record is impeccable. He is absolutely a good God with over 1 billion ways to help His people.

I want to encourage you to look back over your own life and recount the times that you know for a fact that God has delivered you, and pull on those memories to encourage you to live in hope as you expect Him to do the same for you today.

Let me now give you what I call the power of pausing.

The Power of Pausing

I want you to take a deep breath and to pause for a moment to reflect. There are several reasons why I want you to pause. The benefits in pausing are as follows:

1. **Investigation**- Pausing is about finding meaning in each experience

2. **Incubation**- Like Crock-Pot cooking, incubation allows experiences and thoughts to grow to their own full potential

3. **Illumination**- The process of placing value on His performances

4. **Illustration**- The process of expanding your experiences into teachable lessons

I believe that if you would take the time to pause and reflect a moment, it would allow you to investigate, incubate, illuminate, and illustrate the experiences that you've had with your Heavenly

Trusting God In Trouble Times

Father, and those experiences can help you to see

that He's with you during these trouble times.

Let me share with you some Scriptures from the

Bible that will help you to see how powerful it is

to remember your Heavenly Father's track record.

And I said, This *is* my infirmity: *but I will remember* the years of the right hand of the most High. I will remember the works of the LORD: surely I will remember thy wonders of old.

Psalm 77:10,11 (King James Bible)

Remember His marvelous works that He hath done; His wonders, and the judgments of His mouth;

Psalm 105:5 (King James Bible)

I remember the days of old; I meditate on all thy works; I muse on the work of Thy hands.

Psalm 143:5 (King James Bible)

I want to close this chapter by sharing with you something God gave me. He told me to remind His children of several things as it relates to trusting Him. Let me share those with you now. He said that He wants us to trust Him in this manner:

- **Trust His Tenderness**- His heart concerning you

- **Trust His Timing**- His hastening to work on your behalf

- **Trust His Tactics**- His habits of working on behalf of His people

These are the three areas that God is asking you to trust Him. He wants you to know that He is busy working all things out on your behalf. As you read His Bible and see how He delivered the people of old, it is His desire that you would see Him working on your behalf also. His heart toward you is tender and loving. His timing toward you is perfect. His tactics used to bring you out are impeccable, as are His habits. He knows exactly what He's doing, and time will show that He has always been there on your behalf.

Finally, let's look at a few Scriptures that show his track record.

In God will I praise *his* word: in the LORD will I praise *his* word. In God have I put my trust: I will not be afraid what man can do unto me. Thy vows *are* upon me, O God: I will render praises unto thee. For thou hast delivered my soul from death: *wilt* not *thou deliver* my feet from falling, that I may walk before God in the light of the living?

Psalm 56:10-13 (King James Bible)

Trusting God In Trouble Times

Be merciful unto me, O God, be merciful unto me:
for my soul trusteth in thee: yea, in the shadow of
thy wings will I make my refuge, until *these*
calamities be overpast. I will cry unto God most
high; unto God that performeth *all things* for me.

Psalm 57:1,2 (King James Bible)

The steps of a *good* man are ordered by the LORD:
and he delighteth in his way. Though he fall, he
shall not be utterly cast down: for the LORD
upholdeth *him with* his hand. I have been young,
and *now* am old; yet have I not seen the righteous
forsaken, nor his seed begging bread. *He is* ever
merciful, and lendeth; and his seed *is* blessed.

Psalm 37:23-26 (King James Bible)

It is my desire that this chapter has helped you to

remember that you serve a good God, and He is

always there and available to help you through

every problem that you're facing. His track record

is impeccable. All through Scriptures, He has been

there delivering His people through bad times. He stands readily available not only to help you but to comfort you in trouble times.

I think that you are to worship Him for a moment, by telling Him how good He is.

I hope that you would now agree with me that we serve a good God with an impeccable resume of delivering His people in times of trouble.

Conclusion

It is my prayer and my desire that this book has been a source of healing for you, and as you perused through the pages of this book, you have found the strength and the peace that is needed to navigate through life's situations. It is also my prayer and my desire that the words on the pages of this book have been more than just words.

I hope they have leaped from the pages and become one with you and are hidden down in your heart. I hope that the words of this book have become a coach and a mentor for you.

I wrote this book because in our present day, COVID 19, the coronavirus, has swept this country and nation like wildfire, and I see people panicking, fearful, worried, and full of anxiety. I have seen some people hopeless about what tomorrow holds; but, I pray, again, that this book has settled and calmed all of that and has pointed you to the One Who loves you deeply; and, that is Jesus Christ.

I hope you know now that you are not alone; I really hope that you have come to discover that He is right here with you, and for those who already know that, it is my desire that this book served as a coach to simply remind you of the things you may have forgotten or to settle you when days of uncertainties seems to be mounting up against you. I don't know how long you've been quarantined and not allowed to go out, or maybe you have been diagnosed with COVID 19, but I want you to know that there is hope, and there is a brighter future ahead for you. This is not the end. Life is not over. Don't you throw that towel in; don't you wave that flag. Do not surrender. Your best days are ahead of you, and there is still a bright future for you. I am not talking about years from now. I'm talking about right now, even in the midst of all of these uncertainties, even in the midst of COVID 19 or sickness or disease, or calamity that has hit your life. There is a peace and hope that is made readily available for you; and, again, it is my desire that as you went through the chapters of this book, you have discovered all of the things that if applied can help settle you. It can help calm you. It pointed you to a source of strength and power that you are not just existing anymore but that you are ready to thrive and to live your best life.

Beloved, be blessed and know that I'm praying for you even if I don't know you, and I may not even know your name; but, I'm praying for you. You are not alone.

If this book has been a blessing to you, please consider emailing me at kwa@kwa.life and share your testimony.

To find more materials like this, please visit us at www.kwa.life.